FREEDOM
IS FOR FREEING

A Study Book on
Paul's Letter to the Galatians

by Philip Potter
and
Bärbel Wartenberg–Potter

Published by
Mission Education and Cultivation Program Department
for
The Women's Division
General Board of Global Ministries
The United Methodist Church

Published in the United States of America
Library of Congress Catalog Card No. 89-52217

Cover: Illustration by Graphic Design

Please address any critiques or comments about the text to:
Literature Editor, Room 1356, General Board of Global
Ministries. The United Methodist Church, 475 Riverside Drive,
New York, NY 10115.

Table of Contents

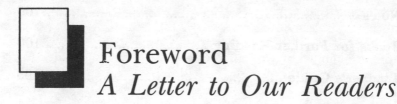

Foreword
A Letter to Our Readers

Do you remember when last you received a really good letter, heartwarming and full of love? Or one with a challenging message, marking your life? Or even a letter of sad rupture and death, but still, a real letter? You might have special places where you keep such letters. Precious memories deserve a special place. And how interesting it is to find old letters after time has passed, and to browse through them, remembering the occasions, the people, the places, be they joyful, hurtful, or lifeturning. Suddenly everything comes back to life. Of course, in a time of telephones, cars and planes, the art of letterwriting has suffered greatly. Many people think: Why write if I can pick up a phone and hear a voice close and lively? Or just take a plane and visit another, in person? But these pleasures of closeness are dearly bought. Often there remain no tangible memories of what was said and felt, and so the past is irretrievable.

But there is also something else. With a special eagerness we tend to read letters addressed to other people, especially those not meant for our eyes. Who has not once broken the law of decency and read someone else's letter; sniffed into the feelings and secrets of another life?

In this study book we want to read with you a letter, written by a man named Saul or Paul, over nineteen hundred years ago, and addressed to people who lived in what is now Central Turkey, in a region called Anatolia. It is an angry letter, to start with; but those who received it were not ashamed of it. For them it was such an important letter in the life of their community that they read it in their meetings of public worship for everyone to hear. They also sent it to other churches for the same reason. Eventually people gathered for posterity (for us) the available letters of Paul, addressed to various churches. Thirteen letters attributed to Paul (although not all written by him personally) are included in what we call today the New Testament. We invite you to read, not a private, but a public letter, written in the first century by Paul, the zealous missionary of Christ, to his early founded churches in Galatia. If it were not for letters like this, we might know very little about the difficulties of the early church. Indeed, if it had not been for letters like this, there might not have been a Christian church at all, only a Christian sect within Judaism with not much influence, and which most likely would have disappeared by now.

In Paul's time, letterwriting was a much more complicated process than now. Letters were written on a precious and expensive material, papyrus, which was processed (sliced and pressed) from the pith of the papyrus plant. The papyrus was engraved with a special pen. Once written, the papyrus pages were put into a leather bag for transport. The laborious process of letterwriting was the only way of communicating between persons separated by long distances, other than sending a messenger. As far as we know, none of the original letters of Paul has survived, only copies. In the early church, many of the letter manuscripts were copied by hand, again and again, and handed down from one generation to the next. This was the primary way of preserving and distributing the letters until printing was invented in the fifteenth century. Somewhere, hidden in earthen vessels in caves and remote places, early copies of letters survived the centuries. Such hiding places were necessary for a church that lived under persecution. The survival of letters from Paul and others gives witness to how precious these letters were to the early church, how well they were kept from sun and storm, water and cold, and persecuting zeal, so that today we may read them and hear the voices of the early witnesses.

You may ask yourself, as many people do: Why do we read this old letter? Of course in the Christian community we are still used to reading the New Testament as a given book, as God's word. But for how many people is this still the case? What would make the angry letter of the man called Paul meaningful for others who are not used either to reading the Bible or to receiving elaborate letters? And even the people in the churches are more used to picking out individual verses in Galatians like "There is no longer Jew or Greek, . . . slave or free, . . . male and female, for you are all one in Christ Jesus" (3:28), or "For freedom Christ has set us free" (5:1). Yes, such sentences speak still to many of us as we live in the Christian tradition. But do we really know what lies behind them and what they imply? We also listen to longer passages of scripture in the Sunday readings at church services. They may be even more clouded in our minds. Why should we study a whole letter with so many strange terms like "circumcision" and "justi-fication," with theological jargon and complicated scriptur-al argumentation? It seems that our church people today are quite satisfied with their present knowledge of the Bible. Careful study and explanation of biblical texts is not a high priority in our lives.

But we live in a world full of dramatic changes and new situations. As Christians we are constantly asked to take stands on newly emerging issues, many of which humanity has created for itself: the search for unlimited growth on a limited earth; the destruction of the environment; the use of scientific knowledge and technology in deadly experi-ments; the threat of the annihilation of the earth; the devastating poverty of two thirds of the world's population, to name only some of a sad and shocking long list. Or closer home: sexual abuse of women and men, growing crime, hunger, drug abuse, destruction of families, racial and cultural conflicts, loss of hope. It is overwhelming to write such lists. Many of these challenges meet us unprepared. And yet, how can we speak about God's redeeming power if we do not apply the "good news" to the "bad situation"? If we do not show in what ways God's purpose with humanity can be seen in light of the scriptures?

Many people think there are no neat answers in the Bible and this is often true. Today's catchwords are not listed among the keywords of the gospel. And yet, it is our conviction that the Bible speaks to and about these issues because it speaks about life and death. It speaks about the forces of evil and sin, but also about God's redemptive power in all ages. Reading the biblical witness will help us to understand more clearly the reality we live in and to recognize the forces at work in it. It will help us to understand our human condition and God's calling. As we see ancient people struggling for answers to the questions of their time, they provide us with their witness and guidance for our time. We may hear God's redeeming voice speaking to us, leading us through the darkness of our time, the "evil age" we live in, and opening us to new vision. Reading the old texts, if we rightly do so, is like looking into a mirror: we see ourselves, our faces, often terribly distorted. But we also see the "new creation," which God made us to be.

Understanding the book of our faith better and exploring it in more depth is the only way we can become mature Christians, not irritated and bewildered by every new question. Hearing about the struggles, mistakes and new beginnings of the young Christian community, hearing their heartbeat, may give life to our own faith.

In this Bible study we deal with a very specific New Testament letter, written by Paul, an apostle. As we start to read, we must take notice of the fact that this letter was read and interpreted by many people before us. In fact, it is one of the texts that inspired the great Reformation led by Martin Luther in the sixteenth century. Paul has been interpreted so much that it is difficult to hear his own voice through all the layers of interpretation over the centuries. No doubt we have benefitted a lot by Paul's interpreters. But he remains a person, loved and praised by many, rejected and scorned by many, claimed and misinterpreted by many. If we are to understand rightly the person who wrote this letter, we have to see him as a man with a particular life experience, living in a certain time and in a certain region of the world. His task, which God had given him, was a very difficult one. In one of his letters he tells us what it meant to be a missionary:

> "Are they ministers of Christ? I am talking like a madman—I am a better one; with far greater labors, far more imprisonments, with countless floggings, and often near death. Five times I have received from the Jews the forty lashes minus one. Three times I was beaten with rods. Once I received a stoning. Three times I was shipwrecked; for a night and a day I was adrift at sea; on frequent journeys, in danger from rivers, danger from bandits, danger from my own people, danger from Gentiles, danger in the city, danger in the wilderness, danger at sea, danger from false brothers and sisters; in toil and hardship, through many a sleepless night, hungry and thirsty, often without food, cold and naked. And, besides other things, I am under daily pressure because of my anxiety for all the churches." (2 Cor. 11:23–28)

Here Paul gets it off his chest: all the fears, tears and pains he went through, from outside but also from within. The letter to the Galatians is one of those documents of deep inner anxiety and distress, but written with a burning heart, yet with feelings of almost motherly tenderness: "My little children, with whom I am again in the pain of childbirth until Christ is formed in you. I wish I were present with you now and could change my [angry] tone [of voice], for I am perplexed about you" (Gal. 4:19–20).

Who is this man who wrote such burning letters? Who is he, the great theologian who inspired Luther and Wesley and many reformers? Can we liberate him from the tomes written about his theology and meet him as a person?

Most knowledge about him comes from his letters, which are full of experiences and stories, and from the Acts of the Apostles. Never does he divorce his life from his thinking and acting. It is all closely knit together. Paul was put many times in prison. And it is believed that he died as a martyr in Rome. This risk, to live as a Christian in the Roman Empire where Christians were persecuted, helped shape his faith, his life and his death.

Levi Oracion, a contemporary prophet from the Philippines writes: "To be ready for death simplifies one's life, purifies one's soul and gives one tremendous courage. It allows for a radical disengagement with the nonessentials of life and frees one for a total commitment to truth." It is in such situations that people experience what a Philippine woman expressed: "I discovered through my detention and torture that I was stronger than I ever dreamt I would be."

Most of us do not have such experiences. Many of us live in "comfortable pews," without being aware of how many Christians today live their faith in very risky circumstances. But it might give us pause to think that Christians in the early church and throughout church history have found themselves put in demanding and uncomfortable situations. The question is not: Why does God put us there? But rather: How do we respond in faith and faithfulness to these demands? Many people grow strong in weak places. Or they grow strong in the midst of crisis. As Christians we are not promised comfortable paths. What we are promised is that God will be beside us on our way. And there is more "life" in life, if we do not avoid its depth and its heights, but "choose life" (Deut. 30:19) and know what we are living for. Paul had one hope: that all who read these letters would become, ourselves, a "living letter of Christ," so that all who do *not* read the Bible anymore, or never read it, can at least read from our very lives God's message of love and faith and justice. Paul invites us to become a letter of Christ to the world: "You yourselves are our letter, written on our hearts, to be known and read by all; and you show that you are a letter of Christ, prepared by us, written not with ink but with the Spirit of the living God, not on tablets of stone, but on tablets of human hearts" (2 Cor. 3:2–3).

Philip Potter
Bärbel Wartenberg–Potter

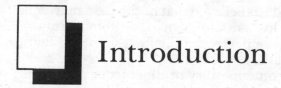

Introduction

Paul and the Churches in Galatia

"He is short of stature, bald and bow–legged, vigorous, with meeting eyebrows and a prominent nose and full of friendliness. Indeed at one moment he looked like a man, and the next he seemed to have the appearance of an angel."

This description of Paul is given in a writing called "Acts of Paul," a legendary narrative of his life.[1] We may glean from it that it was certainly not his beauty that made Paul an impressive person. The opposite seems to be true. In addition to his unimpressive outer appearance, he was even burdened with a chronic affliction that seems to have troubled him lifelong. Many have tried to guess what it might have been, but nobody really knows. So much did he suffer from it that he reminded the Galatians of the state of his health when he first visited them: "My condition put you to the test" (4:14).

But things seemed to change once Paul started to speak. Some real healing and transforming power must have worked in and from him. On his first missionary visit, in Lystra, one of the towns in the Roman province of Galatia, the people even mistook him and Barnabas for Greek gods, Barnabas for Zeus and Paul for Hermes, the messenger of the gods. (See Acts 14:8–13.) They could hardly escape from being worshipped and given sacrifices by the local priests, so powerful was their presence. Paul won the hearts of the people as he talked and even the Galatians, whom he rebukes in our letter, were really deeply attracted to him. "If possible, you would have plucked out your eyes and given them to me" (4:14).

A Hellenistic Jew

Paul was born in Tarsus, a small commercial and university town in Asia Minor, located right at the crossing of main travel routes. At the beginning of the first century, it was a center of considerable traffic, connecting the Hellenistic (Greek) world with the Semitic countries. Paul was therefore early exposed to different languages, different cultures and religions. He grew up in a community of Hellenistic Jews and was himself born and brought up as a Jew.

From about 500 B.C., after the Babylonian exile, Jews had begun to migrate from the land of Israel, entering trade and commerce in the wider Mediterranean. After the conquests of Alexander the Great (333 B.C.), they had even adopted the common language, the *"Koine"*—Greek, and translated their Bible into Greek. It was called the Septuagint and was the Greek version of what we Christians call the Old Testament. Through their contacts with Jewish people, some Greeks became converts to the Jewish faith. Intermarriages became possible, but male converts were expected to be circumcised to come into full membership in the Jewish community, and the Jews of the dispersion (diaspora) kept their ties with Palestine and Jerusalem. On the whole, Hellenistic Jews would have a different outlook on the world from that of the Jews of Palestine. They had to live in a cultural climate of diversity and in the wider world of Egypt, Persia, Arabia, Greece and Rome. All these cultures mingled and created their own cosmopolitan atmosphere. Paul was exposed to all that.

A Roman Citizen

At the same time, according to Acts, Paul was a Roman citizen. The citizenship gave him special privileges and protection. For example, he could only be tried by a proper Roman court (Acts 25:10–12) and certain forms of punishment were not practiced against Roman citizens (*e.g.* execution was allowed only by the sword).

Not everybody living in the Roman Empire was automatically a citizen. It was a special privilege. However, the Roman Empire had unified the Mediterranean world by giving it a common legal code, a common coinage, and common weight and measurement systems. Through the frequent movement of troops, a very effective system of roads and transport had developed, which allowed Paul to travel. In this context the Christian faith would spread more easily. For instance, long before Paul was taken to Rome, Christians were living already in Rome.

As a Roman citizen one was obligated to worship before the idol of the Roman Emperor. Jewish people were exempted officially from this duty.

It is unlikely that Paul would have become the great Christian missionary if his home had not been in this wider Judaism, if he had not been able to read and write Greek and possess the Septuagint as his Bible, if he had not been used to accommodating himself to foreign customs, and if he had not had an eye for the wider world of highways by land and sea and for the great cities of the Mediterranean world.[2]

Paul the Pharisee

It is not enough, however, to describe Paul as a Hellenistic Jew and a Roman citizen. First of all he had been raised in the tradition of the faith of his ancestors. He had become a Pharisee. The Judaism of Paul's time was very diverse and we do not have sufficient knowledge about it. The historian Josephus of Rome and the philosopher Philo of Alexandria are our main sources of knowledge of Hellenistic Judaism. In recent years the discovery of the Dead Sea scrolls of Qumran has shed new light on the diversity of Judaism in

Jesus' time. We can discern the following groups:

Scribes, who studied and taught the law.

Pharisees, who lived a specially pious life and ensured the keeping of the law.

Sadducees, the priestly nobility.

Am–ha'arez, "the people of the land," people of ordinary and poorer origin who often could not, because of the demands of daily life, afford to fulfill the whole law. Jesus and his disciples belonged to this group.

In order to be a proper Jew one had first of all to be circumcised (Gen. 17:10 ff.) and keep the laws of the Torah, *e.g.* the food laws, Sabbath regulations and the feast days of the Jewish calendar. All of these were contained in the first five books of the Bible (the Pentateuch). After the Babylonian exile, more and more emphasis was put on the strict observance of the law and many additional regulations came into existence. Jews traditionally thought of the Torah as having 613 laws. For ordinary people, by the time of Jesus, the law had become a kind of entangling labyrinth.

To understand Paul, it is important to know that already in the prophetic time of the Old Testament, and even before, there was strong disapproval of a superficial and legalistic use of the law. The priests and prophets spoke about the "circumcision of the heart" (Deut. 10:16 and Jer. 4:4), thus pointing towards the inner attitude rather than the outer observance of the law.

Paul belonged by birth and by education to three different worlds: the world of Hellenistic Jews, the world of the Roman Empire, and the world of Pharisaic tradition connected with Jerusalem.

Time of the Letter to the Galatians

Paul's letter to the Galatians is one of the earliest writings of the New Testament. We have to understand that the four Gospels were written only in the last third of the first century when nearly all of the eyewitnesses of Jesus' life had died. (They grew out of a need to fix in writing the stories of Jesus' lifetime.) Paul's letters, although they address the situation after Jesus' death, were written earlier than the Gospels that report Jesus' lifetime. Galatians was most likely written between A.D. 50 and 55.

Theme of the Letter

Since the early church after Pentecost was largely made up of Jewish Christians, the question was: What role should the law of Moses (the Torah) play in the new movement? Was it still necessary to become a Jew before becoming a Christian? This is one of the main themes of the letter.

The letter is written in a fighting spirit. Paul could write very affirmative letters, like the one to the Philippians. But in this letter he has to face a crucial problem of the early church. When he had first preached in Galatia, he found strong and enthusiastic support among the Galatians (4:14–15), and a congregation was formed. But after some time people came who "confused" the Galatians. They were trying to persuade the Galatians to accept the law of Moses and circumcision in addition to the gospel of Christ. These outsiders represented a faction in the Jerusalem church. We do not have much certain knowledge about them, but they obviously firmly believed that every Christian must first adhere to the Jewish law. We also do not know these opponents in person. But Paul responds in his letter to a number of their accusations and arguments.

Style of the Letter

Sometimes Paul's arguments are very difficult to understand without knowing what points, raised by his opponents, he was addressing. It is like receiving answers without knowing the questions. We can only guess from the answers what the arguments must have been. As a Pharisee

Paul was used to scriptural argumentation. As a man with a Hellenistic education he was used to rhetorical methods of arguing. Both come to bear in his writings. However, even if not every argument in the letter can clearly be explained, this letter stands out more for the firm testimony it gives about the nature of the gospel than for the details of the argument.

About Galatia

Paul writes to the "churches" in Galatia. This is the only time in his correspondence that Paul addresses several congregations or Christian communities. This might suggest an intensive missionary effort by him and his helpers, covering a wide area. The Acts of the Apostles do not give any account of a mission to Galatia, except to Iconium, Lystra and Derbe during what is often described as Paul's first missionary tour (Acts 14:1–23). These cities in Lyconia were attached by the Romans to Galatia in 25 B.C. to form "the province of Galatia." However, we are informed that on two occasions Paul went "through the region of Phrygia and Galatia" (Acts 16:6; 18:23). So he knew well the churches in the region or country of Galatia. What was the region of Galatia?

Now known as the central plateau of Turkey around the present capital, Ankara (in Paul's time, Ancyra, capital of Galatia), this region was occupied by the Hittites as early as the second millenium B.C. By 279 B.C. Celtic tribes had come in from the West. They were a very warlike people, and were often used by local princes as mercenaries for plundering cities and taking land. By 189 B.C., the emerging Roman Empire defeated them in battle and made their country a protectorate. Over the years the Celts mixed with the surrounding peoples and, culturally, they were both Hellenized and Romanized, though in the rural areas they still spoke Celtic dialects. It was to this region of Galatia (same as Gaul) and this very mixed people in race, culture and religion that Paul first went with the gospel of freedom in Christ.

We can therefore say that Paul's letter addressed the churches in the country of Galatia as well as those in the Lyconia area—all of which came under one jurisdiction, the province of Galatia. These churches were Gentile in membership, but used the Greek Old Testament for their instruction. When Peter was later writing a letter to the churches in Asia Minor, he mentioned Galatia (1 Pet. 1:1).

Content of the Letter

In our Bibles the letter to the Galatians is divided into six chapters. We will read chapter by chapter. The first two chapters have a strong emphasis on Paul's personal life. Chapters 3 and 4 expand the theological argumentation. Chapters 5 and 6 speak about the consequences of the gospel and the life in the community.

Try to read the whole letter through, making notes and marking your questions and thoughts. Only if you are acquainted with the text, will you benefit from the detailed explanations. It is an act of love of the Scripture to be patient with it.

1. Angry Astonishment

Galatians

1 Paul an apostle—sent neither by human commission nor from human authorities, but through Jesus Christ and God the Father, who raised him from the dead— ²and all the members of God's family who are with me, To the churches of Galatia:

3 Grace to you and peace from God our Father and the Lord Jesus Christ, ⁴who gave himself for our sins to set us free from the present evil age, according to the will of our God and Father, ⁵to whom be the glory forever and ever. Amen.

6 I am astonished that you are so quickly deserting the one who called you in the grace of Christ and are turning to a different gospel— ⁷not that there is another gospel, but there are some who are confusing you and want to pervert the gospel of Christ. ⁸But even if we or an angel from heaven should proclaim to you a gospel contrary to what we proclaimed to you, let that one be accursed! ⁹As we have said before, so now I repeat, if anyone proclaims to you a gospel contrary to what you received, let that one be accursed!

10 Am I now seeking human approval, or God's approval? Or am I trying to please people? If I were still pleasing people, I would not be a servant of Christ.

11 For I want you to know, brothers and sisters, that the gospel that was proclaimed by me is not of human origin; ¹²for I did not receive it from a

human source, nor was I taught it, but I received it through a revelation of Jesus Christ.

13 You have heard, no doubt, of my earlier life in Judaism. I was violently persecuting the church of God and was trying to destroy it. [14]I advanced in Judaism beyond many among my people of the same age, for I was far more zealous for the traditions of my ancestors. [15]But when God, who had set me apart before I was born and called me through his grace, was pleased [16]to reveal his Son to me, so that I might proclaim him among the Gentiles, I did not confer with any human being, [17]nor did I go up to Jerusalem to those who were already apostles before me, but I went away at once into Arabia, and afterwards I returned to Damascus.

18 Then after three years I did go up to Jerusalem to visit Cephas and stayed with him fifteen days; [19]but I did not see any other apostle except James the Lord's brother. [20]In what I am writing to you, before God, I do not lie! [21]Then I went into the regions of Syria and Cilicia, [22]and I was still unknown by sight to the churches of Judea that are in Christ; [23]they only heard it said, "The one who formerly was persecuting us is now proclaiming the faith he once tried to destroy." [24]And they glorified God because of me.

Greetings from an Apostle (1:1–5)

The letter starts with his name, "Paul," and his position, "Apostle," which means one who is sent with a commission and given full responsibility and trust by the sending person. He was a kind of "ambassador extraordinary," a "high commissioner," not just a simple employee. He is not talking of things human beings invent; nor is he sent by human persons (for instance the apostles in Jerusalem). The highest authority has sent him, "Jesus Christ and God the

Father." At the very beginning Paul puts all the emphasis on his <u>divine calling</u> and his proper authority, invoking the resurrected Christ. He hands in his credentials, so to speak, and they are of highest caliber and not easily challenged (1:1).

But he does not write alone. There is a community around him of others who share in his ministry and help him, for example, to write this letter. They certainly share his concerns. Paul's work is always within and sustained by a community. There is <u>no individualism in faith</u> or in leadership (1:2).

The letter is written not just to one church, but to several churches in the province of Galatia. Paul greets them with a solemn greeting, almost a prayer. Maybe this formula was used in their worship services. Often liturgical texts find their way into the flow of a letter. Paul wishes them "<u>grace</u>," which means "the selfgiving love of God" and "<u>peace</u>" ("shalom"), the inner and outer wellbeing of the community (1:3). ("Shalom" was and is a familiar greeting in the Jewish community.)

There follows now one of the oldest formulas for the meaning of Jesus' death: the <u>selfgiving sacrifice of Christ for humanity</u>. "Christ who gave himself for our sins." By Christ's redemptive death, humanity has been given a new chance to live a new life, to live differently, not to follow compulsively the evil powers in and around us. We are freed, liberated, delivered to live a life of goodness, outside the constraints of evil that mark every age in a different and unique way (see also 4:3–11).

We are not promised to be taken *out* of this world as some people read this, but to be able <u>to live outside the gripping</u>, seducing power of <u>evil forces</u> that could keep us in bondage: fear, oppression, guilt, lack of confidence, greed, selfishness, injustice. "To set us free from the present evil age" (1:4).

This is God's will and best intention for us and reason enough to praise God with a form of doxology: "to whom be the glory for ever and ever" (1:5).

3

Confusion (1:6–10)

Paul is astonished about the Galatians. They who had been so enthusiastic and affectionate with him were quickly ready to change their allegiance. Paul equates their behavior with deserting God: "Deserting the one who has called you." They had run into the other camp, the camp of Paul's opponents. Had they already accepted the teaching of those opponents or did Paul write because things were still open? The Galatians had turned to "a different gospel" (1:6).

Paul corrects himself: there is not really a different gospel because accepting the law of Moses would nullify the true gospel (2:21). If people still had to undergo the burden of obeying the many rules and regulations of the law, if they were still to fulfill the letter of the law rather than live in the freedom of the gospel, then "grace" itself was no longer valid. It was no longer the message.

Paul had no compromising word for this position or for his opponents. Since they confused the Galatians and perverted the gospel, changed its direction, the strongest words were necessary (1:7).

Here, the full weight of Paul's anger comes out. He goes so far as to say that even if he himself should tell them something different, or an angel from heaven, such a one should be cursed (1:8). Curse meaning excommunication, "cutting someone off from the community." Two times he throws his curse out and since in ancient times it was believed that a curse became effective once it was written or spoken, and the conditions were fulfilled, a very serious situation is created. Since the issue at stake is of such importance for their faith, the curse assumes even more weight. It becomes a "sacred curse," a "cutting off," "anathema" (1:9). (See I Cor. 5:3–5 and 9–13 for similar "excommunications.")

So the beginning of Paul's letter is very dramatic. A "holy curse" is hanging like a dark cloud over the whole letter or rather over the Galatian churches. Paul says: I am not a

4

magic or religious sorcerer who persuades God or people with magic quackery. Nor am I going to please you Galatians. <u>Because to "please people," to say whatever is just nice for their ears, is an attitude that no Christian should ever take</u>. He calls himself literally a "slave of Christ," by which he expresses his total devotion and commitment (1:10).

<u>Receiving a Revelation (1:11, 12)</u>

Paul puts in verses 11 and 12 all his eloquence again on the same matter. The gospel he proclaims is not his own or anybody's invention. He has not received it "secondhand," not from hearsay or somebody's instruction. <u>It is his own experience with the risen Christ</u> (1:12).

Paul insists that the gospel he preaches came to him direct as a "revelation from Christ." God intervened in his life and this speaks for itself. The revelation of which he speaks had Christ at its center. This does not mean the visual and audible appearance of Christ. It was not like a television screen where one looks at it and recognizes the face. Rather, the deep and true inner meaning of the life and death of Christ became clear, obvious, self–explanatory to Paul. He looked at the same reality that others had observed, that is that Jesus, the executed Jew, was claimed to be the Messiah.

As if a veil had been removed, this reality <u>appeared</u> now to him in its true light, <u>in divine light</u>. This truth took hold of him and became the driving power of his life everafter. The inner event was initiated by an outer event. A bright light from heaven reached him. This is how Acts described it (Acts 9:3). Many people in biblical times and even today describe such experiences, such revelations in their lives, and they see God's hand at work in them. <u>Unexpected,</u> and with <u>overwhelming power</u>, this revelation changed Paul's life.

This experience with the risen Christ was shaking off the fear and self–protection and making out of the persecutor the man who eventually would become a martyr for Christ.

5

Conversion: What Is It?

The ninth chapter of Acts tells us about Paul's conversion on the Damascus Road. He refers to that conversion in the first chapter of Galatians. A dramatic event in his life, it is not at all glorious, but shattering and dangerous. Blindness falls upon him and persecution follows after. The hallmark of this conversion is a complete change in his thinking and living. Nothing is smooth or easy about it.

In the Christian community many different experiences of conversion exist. Many people are reluctant to talk about their conversion—others speak easily and frequently about it, indeed insist that one must be "born again" in a certain way. But it does not necessarily come over convincingly to me. What is your experience?

A "revelation" that leads to a "conversion" is something very intimate and personal. Many people do not want to speak loudly or boastfully about these moments when new life begins to be formed in us. The encounter with God does not always come with majestic manifestations. Elijah did not encounter God in the storm, nor in the earthquake, nor in the fire, but heard God in a "small voice" (1 Kings 19:11–12). It comes often like a "thief in the night" into our lives, rests like a seed in our hearts for a long while before it grows to be seen, named and noticed. The Bible provides us with many different examples of "conversions" and we therefore do not need to press them into one single mold.

But one thing is clear: A true conversion always leaves recognizable traces behind. Suddenly or slowly, life turns in another direction.

I am one of those persons who prefer not to speak quickly about my "conversion" story. If I have to tell it,

I have to tell several stories. I would begin like the church father Augustine began his story. He saw in a quiet hour a book lying on a table and he was told: "Take and read!" What he took was the Bible and he read Romans 13:13 and 14. For me the book I picked up was a small paperback containing the speeches and resolutions of the World Council of Churches' Fourth Assembly at Uppsala in 1968. Barbara Ward, Kenneth Kaunda and James Baldwin were some of the people who talked to me from those pages about God's justice and human injustice. They talked about a world full of affluence and hunger; about one of the first slave ships carrying its desperate load from Africa to the Americas, called "The Good Ship Jesus." It was a shocking and shaming and challenging conversion. I saw before me the bloated bellies of hungry children in Africa and the segregated townships in South Africa, which I was later to visit. Some voice asked me: "What are you going to do about it? Will you allow the name of Christ to be so distorted, abused and perverted in this world? Will you be a minister of God's good news to such situations? Or will you be part of a comfortable church that is silent about these things?"

This slow and steadily progressing conversion made an angry person out of me, angry about injustice, angry about silence, angry about my own and others' "slowness of heart." A lot of trouble awaited me in my church, in my private and public life after this. But it was also exhilarating: to find new friends, to have good arguments and proof in the encounters, to discover the Bible in a new and meaningful way. The more I read it with new eyes, the more it began to speak to me.—*B.W.P.*

Violent Persecution, but . . . (1:13–17)

How sudden the change and how far–reaching the consequences. They can only be measured by knowing Paul's life
before the event. In Acts of the Apostles we hear more
about Paul's former life in Judaism (1:13). The Galatians
obviously knew the story. Paul was a witness to the famous
speech by Stephen before the Sanhedrin in Jerusalem.
Stephen was a Greek–speaking Hellenistic Jew who had
been elected by the church in Jerusalem and commissioned
by the apostles to distribute food more equitably among the
various communities of Christian widows in Jerusalem
(Acts 6:1–6). In his speech before the highpriest, Stephen
had led the Jews through the whole course of their own
history, concluding from it that "the Most High does not
dwell in houses made by hands." This was an attack on the
Jerusalem temple and was meant to convey the message
that God cannot be limited to *one* place and to *one* people
only.

Stephen also denounced those "who received the law and
did not keep it," and continued, "you stiff–necked people,
uncircumcised in heart and ears, you always resist the Holy
Spirit. As your fathers did, so do you" (Acts 7:48–53).
Stephen further accused the Jews of having betrayed and
murdered the "righteous one," Jesus Christ. Paul, then still
bearing his Jewish name Saul, was present when they cast
Stephen out of the city and stoned him. "And the witnesses
laid their garments at Saul's feet" (Acts 7:58).

After Stephen had become the first martyr, a "great
persecution arose against the church in Jerusalem. And
they were all scattered throughout the region of Judea and
Samaria, except the apostles. But Saul was ravaging the
church by entering house after house; dragging off both
men and women, he committed them to prison" (Acts
8:1–3). During this persecution people went as far as Antioch and began to build new Christian communities of Jews
and Gentiles (Acts 11:19).

These were the violent ways Paul speaks about in Galatians 1:13. As a pious Jew, he was zealous for his ancestors' tradition (1:14). He could not accept the thought that this Jesus of Nazareth had so radically reinterpreted the law. (As seen in the Sermon on the Mount: "You have heard that it was said . . . *but I say to you,*" Mt. 5:21ff.) Why had he bypassed the most faithful of all, the Scribes and Pharisees, and turned to the people on the margin, the poor people, the fisherfolk and shepherds? Paul, more than most of his contemporaries, was committed to the Jewish faith. His whole upbringing and education had directed him that way.

But God had long been reaching out for him. That is how Paul sees it. God had chosen him before he was born (1:15). This strong sense of calling seems to be present in people who have an especially difficult task to fulfill in life. Therefore it is not surprising that Paul's words resemble the words spoken by God to the great Hebrew prophet Jeremiah: "Before I formed you in the womb I knew you . . . I appointed you a prophet to the nations" (Jer. 1:5; see also Is. 49:5, 6).

Invoking the prophetic calling and commissioning of Jeremiah, who was an outcast priest, Paul, the outsider apostle, puts himself in the great and daring tradition of Hebrew faith. Jeremiah was the prophet who had already criticized the legalistic use of the law and announced the coming of a new covenant. "I will put my law within them, write it upon their hearts" (Jer. 31:31–34). The prophetic courage to say unpopular things, to confront the mighty and the religious and to fight for God's truth, is a hallmark of Paul's ministry and makes clear that he stood firmly rooted in the best of Jewish tradition. It is God's grace that makes daring people.

The story following Stephen's death in Acts 8 and 9 shows the outer events in Paul's life (also Acts 22:14–16; Acts 26:9–18; Phil. 3:3–8).

In the middle of his persecution activities something happened to Paul. A light and a voice from heaven struck him down on his way from Jerusalem to Damascus. The

9

voice called him into accountability. "Saul, Saul, why do you persecute me?" He understood it to be the voice of Jesus. This was a type of question that does not so much aim at an answer, as turn a person inward to search and ponder the whole purpose of his or her life: What am I doing? Was it only by persecuting others that Saul hoped to find fulfillment in life and peace with God? Was his life to be spent in the destruction of innocent people who had heard the voice of God in this Christ, and were doing no harm, but living differently from the prescribed traditions?

Paul does not tell all this in the letter. He describes to the Galatians only the inner way he was led. God called him "through his grace," through a loving act of attention for this undeserving zealous persecutor. God turned his life around by leading him to a deep inner encounter with Christ (1:16). Paul understood that a new way of life and faith had been opened for all humanity, Jews and Gentiles alike, through this "improbable" Messiah Jesus.

But this conversion had a purpose. Paul did not conceive it only as an extraordinary religious experience. God made him the person who would go to the Gentiles (1:16). The early church considered itself as a movement within the Jewish faith, related first and mainly to the "chosen people." But Paul saw himself especially commissioned to go to the Gentiles with a greater vision: that there be an inclusive community for Jews and Gentiles, shaped by the love of Christ and love of one another, extending to the ends of the whole inhabited earth, the *oikoumene* and even to the whole creation (Rom. 8:18–22).

This calling was stark and unique. It was not the hour to expose or discuss it with anybody, but to let it sink into his life with all its weight. Shock and shame, bewilderment and joy must have been part of it. Paul tried to come to terms with all of this. Therefore, he did not consult with anybody (1:16). The only thing we hear is, "he was baptized and took food and was strengthened" (Acts 9:18–19).

He did not hurry to Jerusalem to the other apostles and seek their approval. Instead he went to Arabia, a desert region (1:17). He does not say what he did there. Maybe he spent some time by himself, meditating in the desert as Jesus did at the beginning of his ministry. Perhaps there he started to work out his missionary message. But afterwards he returned to Damascus, the place of his conversion, from which he had fled from the Jews under threat of his life (Acts 9:23–24).

Visit to Jerusalem (1:18–24)

Paul's aim with this letter is to win back the Galatians. He wants to assure them that *his* gospel is standing firm in its own right. To this end he continues to tell episodes of his life.

Only three years after his conversion he paid his first visit to Jerusalem. He reports that he met with Cephas (which is the Hebrew name for Peter, the "rock") who was then obviously a leading apostle (1:18). He also met James, "the brother of our Lord," another church leader or "pillar" of the church (1:19).

The visit was short and it seems that Paul met primarily with the two main leaders. He did not meet the other apostles; we do not know why. But the visit did not make him in any way dependent on Jerusalem for his "authority." So concerned is he about making this clear that he swears: "Before God, I do not lie" (1:20). His opponents in Galatia must have belittled him as being only a secondary authority, who sought advice and instructions from the Jerusalem apostles. They possibly declared his gospel as inferior to theirs. Since Paul had never encountered Jesus of Nazareth during his earthly ministry, he maintained a difficult stance over against the original eleven disciples. That is why he pulls all his weight to prove his independent authority and his commissioning by Christ himself.

His itinerary continues to Syria and Cilicia, far away from Jerusalem, but in the area he himself came from, Tarsus (1:21), certainly an act of bravery.

11

The churches in Judea did not know him by sight. He kept a distance. Incidentally, Paul is the oldest witness of the existence of churches in Judea. Paul introduces a kind of "hearsay," which had gone around about him: "The one who once was persecuting us, is now proclaiming the faith he once tried to destroy" (1:22–23). The words of Jesus at Damascus come to mind: "Why do you persecute me"? The persecution of the early church equals the persecution of Christ himself.

The loss of such a fierce enemy as Saul and the gain of Paul as a fervent witness gave the Christian community reason for great relief. So the chapter ends with this sigh of relief and thanksgiving to God by the hard–pressed early church. "They glorified God because of me" (1:24). God had shown goodness and mercy by liberating the Christians from a persecutor, and not only liberating them, but adding the persecutor to their numbers.

2. Conflict in the Church

Galatians

2 Then after fourteen years I went up again to Jerusalem with Barnabas, taking Titus along with me. ²I went up in response to a revelation. Then I laid before them (though only in a private meeting with the acknowledged leaders) the gospel that I proclaim among the Gentiles, in order to make sure that I was not running, or had not run, in vain. ³But even Titus, who was with me, was not compelled to be circumcised, though he was a Greek. ⁴But because of false believers secretly brought in, who slipped in to spy on the freedom we have in Christ Jesus, so that they might enslave us— ⁵we did not submit to them even for a moment, so that the truth of the gospel might always remain with you. ⁶And from those who were supposed to be acknowledged leaders (what they actually were makes no difference to me; God shows no partiality) —those leaders contributed nothing to me. ⁷On the contrary, when they saw that I had been entrusted with the gospel for the uncircumcised, just as Peter had been entrusted with the gospel for the circumcised ⁸(for he who worked through Peter making him an apostle to the circumcised also worked through me in sending me to the Gentiles), ⁹and when James and Cephas and John, who were acknowledged pillars, recognized the grace that had been given to me, they gave to Barnabas and me the right hand of fellowship, agreeing that we should go to the Gentiles and they to the circumcised. ¹⁰They

asked only one thing, that we remember the poor, which was actually what I was eager to do.

11 But when Cephas came to Antioch, I opposed him to his face, because he stood self–condemned; [12]for until certain people came from James, he used to eat with the Gentiles. But after they came, he drew back and kept himself separate for fear of the circumcision faction. [13]And the other Jews joined him in this hypocrisy, so that even Barnabas was led astray by their hypocrisy. [14]But when I saw that they were not acting consistently with the truth of the gospel, I said to Cephas before them all, "If you, though a Jew, live like a Gentile and not like a Jew, how can you compel the Gentiles to live like Jews?"

15 We ourselves are Jews by birth and not Gentile sinners; [16]yet we know that a person is justified not by the works of the law but through faith in Jesus Christ. And we have come to believe in Christ Jesus, so that we might be justified by faith in Christ, and not by doing the works of the law, because no one will be justified by the works of the law. [17]But if, in our effort to be justified in Christ, we ourselves have been found to be sinners, is Christ then a servant of sin? Certainly not! [18]But if I build up again the very things that I once tore down, then I demonstrate that I am a transgressor. [19]For through the law I died to the law, so that I might live to God. I have been crucified with Christ; [20]and it is no longer I who live, but it is Christ who lives in me. And the life I now live in the flesh I live by faith in the Son of God, who loved me and gave himself for me. [21]I do not nullify the grace of God; for if justification comes through the law, then Christ died for nothing.

A Difficult Meeting (Jerusalem Council: 2:1–9)

If we think the life of the early Christians was harmonious except for pressures from outside, we deceive ourselves. There was persecution from outside and there were divisions inside. Paul continues to tell the Galatians the story of his life; but now we are going to hear of the deep struggles the early Christians had to undergo in order to find their way.

After fourteen years Paul went up again to Jerusalem, this time with Barnabas and Titus (2:1). About Barnabas we hear in Acts 11:22 that he was sent from Jerusalem to Antioch to look into the situation of a rapidly growing Christian community. It was he who went to Tarsus to look out for Paul. And he brought Paul to Antioch, obviously introducing him into this flourishing community. Both worked together for a long time in the first missionary journey. Later they parted over a disagreement (Acts 15:36–41). The background of the journey of Paul and Barnabas to Jerusalem is the following. The number of Gentile Christians had been steadily growing in Asia Minor. Since the Jewish Christians considered the new movement to be within the ethical and religious boundaries of Judaism, the question was raised as to whether the new converts had to keep the Mosaic law.

"People from Judea," the province in which Jerusalem is located, had come to Antioch, which was the main center of missionary activity among Gentiles (Acts 13:1–3).These people from Judea were teaching that circumcision was necessary for every male believer. Circumcision stands out as the single most important sign of being a Jewish male. It stood for Jewish religious identity.

Within Judaism, circumcision, a small operation performed on the penis of the male child, normally takes place on the eighth day after birth (Gen. 17:10–14). The operation may have had both hygienic and cultic origins. The story given in Exodus 4:25–26 is extremely difficult to explain; but as it is performed on the male sexual organ,

15

this rite seems to give a special symbolic significance to the male procreative power. This, however, was not the explicit meaning in the Jewish rite, which was and is introduced in the name of Abraham "as a sign of the covenant" between God and Israel (Gen. 17:ll). Male Jewish Christians were still circumcised Jews and the question was whether this rite was essential for all male believers as well. Besides circumcision, there were numerous cultic and other laws that pious Jews observed.

Paul and Barnabas strongly disagreed with the idea of imposing circumcision in the Gentile church in Antioch (Acts 15:2). The church decided to send the two of them to Jerusalem to clarify the matter. We should note that the account of the event in Acts 15 does not fully coincide with Paul's account in Galatians, but Paul's report preceded Acts by about twenty years. Paul tells us that he and Barnabas took along Titus, a Greek who, because he was uncircumcised (2:1), represented the case of the Gentile Christians.

To show his independent action, Paul again stresses that he went "in response to revelation," not because anybody had ordered or pressed him to go (2:2). In the meeting, which was later to be called the "Jerusalem Council" and which took place with the acknowledged leaders, Paul unfolded what he had been teaching to the Gentiles: his doctrine of God's love in Christ, which made circumcision superfluous. He did so out of concern for the churches he had formed among the Gentiles. They all lived according to his teaching, but were now threatened by his opponents' insistence on circumcision and rituals. His many years of missionary work, his credibility and, as he was convinced, the truth of the gospel of Jesus Christ, were at stake (2:2). The case of Titus provides evidence of the outcome of the meeting. Titus was *not* forced to be circumcised in Jerusalem (2:3). But the meeting itself was difficult.

False believers had come into the meeting to trap Paul and unmask him as the one who neglected the Jewish heritage. Perhaps he did not keep certain food regulations out of solidarity with the Gentile believers. His "freedom in

Christ," his liberated attitude towards these religious practices, were a thorn in their side. Paul does not spare them strong language: "to spy out our freedom" (2:4). But he did "not submit to them even for a moment" (2:5). His conviction that no Gentile must submit to the requirements of the Jewish laws, in order to be Christian, stood firm and unbending. He adopted this firm attitude "so that the truth of the gospel might always remain with you" (2:5). Here now he turns the reporting on the meeting into a plea to the Galatians not to give in to the pressures of the Christian Jews who wanted to continue to keep the law, in the same way that he had not given in to the pillars of the church in Jerusalem.

The position of the acknowledged leaders in the Jerusalem Council was different from the position of the "false believers" (2:4). As Jews they would stick to their Jewish heritage, but would not impose it on the Gentiles. Therefore, they did not make any requirement or imposition on Paul in the meeting. Paul speaks with some careful wording about their leadership positions by making sure that he does not present them as superior to him. "God shows no partiality" (2:6).

His presentation must have impressed everybody. It became evident that he had a special gift, a "charisma," for preaching the gospel to the uncircumcised. This gospel must have been somewhat different from what Peter was preaching to the circumcised. Note that Paul regards himself and Peter as being on equal footing (2:7, 8).

At this point we must remember Cephas's (Peter's) life story. He was one of the twelve disciples of Jesus, a fisherman from Galilee, also called Simon. He was the one to name Jesus first as "Messiah," or "Christ." But when it came to the trial of Jesus, it was also he who betrayed and deserted Jesus miserably. When challenged by one of the maidservants, he denied that he had ever known Jesus. He could not take much pride in this experience. After the Resurrection, he was one of the disciples to see the risen Christ early and as John tells us, he was commissioned by

Christ "to tend the flock" (Jn. 21:15–19).

In one sense he did not have a real advantage over Paul, who also was commissioned, only by revelation. But Peter rose to extraordinary leadership at Pentecost and afterwards, although he always remained a simple fisherman (Acts 4:13) who had not studied the law like Paul the Pharisee. As we see these two important leaders of the early church, Paul and Peter, we recognize that both of them had received their calling from God through Christ (2:7, 8).

Only at this point Paul mentions three names, James, Cephas and John. This might indicate that the leadership comprised now not only Cephas (Peter), but indeed three persons, with James, the brother of Jesus, occupying the position of honor. Paul seems to be deliberate in pointing out to the Galatians that the Jerusalem Council had recognized his theological soundness and dedicated work, the "grace that had been given" to him. In a formal act of agreement the Council acknowledged Paul's and Barnabas' position as legitimate and gave them the "right hand of fellowship," confirming their division of labor (2:9).

"Remember the Poor" (2:10)

Paul mentions now the only condition, or rather petition, made by Jerusalem leaders, "that we remember the poor, which was actually what I was eager to do" (2:10).

Remembering the poor was not just a nontheological point, added to the otherwise theological debate. It had its deep inner connection with the issues raised. Who were the poor and what does "remember" mean?

The groups who made up the first Christian community in Jerusalem had been drawn from the followers of Jesus, who were fishermen and country people. We do not know about their means of subsistence in the time after Jesus' death. The petition in the Lord's Prayer, "Give us this day our daily bread," seems to indicate that people were not assured of every day's bread. The followers of Jesus certainly were not wealthy and highly respected socially (Acts 4:13). In the Hellenistic towns of Asia Minor, the new converts seem to have come from a mixed social background with some fairly well–off people among them. We know that some communities sustained the apostle Paul during his visits, whereas in others he had to work for his own living. A special poverty among the Jerusalem Christians and those in Judea was possibly connected with periods of drought and famine in the area (Acts 11:27–30).

To remember the poor did not mean only to think and pray about poverty but to *do* something about it. Paul gave the following advice (to the Corinthians): "On the first day of every week, each of you is to put aside and save whatever extra you earn, so that collections need not be taken when I come. And when I arrive, I will send any whom you approve with letters to take your gift to Jerusalem" (1 Cor. 16:1–3).

Titus, Paul's coworker, was put in charge of the collection in Corinth (2 Cor. 8:6), but we know that collections had also been made in Galatia and other places. Paul reminds the Corinthians of their intention to send the collection: " . . . it is a question of fair balance between your present abundance and their need, so that their abundance may be for your need in order that there may be a fair balance" (2 Cor. 8:14). Paul writes two chapters about the theological significance of this donation. In 2 Corinthians 8 and 9 he envisages the readiness of sharing with the poor churches as a "harvest of your righteousness" (2 Cor. 9:10), as a showing of love. His reminder comes "not as a command," but "testing the genuineness of your love" (2 Cor. 8:8). On this matter the equal sharing with the poor is an outpouring of genuine love, which responds to the love of Christ. "For you know the generous act of our Lord Jesus Christ, that though he was rich, yet for your sakes he became poor, so that by his poverty you might become rich" (2 Cor. 8:9).

From Paul's whole understanding of the gospel, care and concern for each other, generosity and sharing are central expressions of faith. Therefore, he welcomes the opportunity to show that his understanding of the gospel has already naturally embraced the cause of the poor. It is not an afterthought, as it is in many churches (and even in most commentaries about Galatians), for Paul was "eager to do it." Another aspect is also important: This sharing with the poorer Jerusalem church was in Paul's thinking a bond, which tied the Christian community together in spite of the many differences and emerging divisions. This collection helped to keep the doors open. In this respect, the unity was better maintained by a concrete action of faith than by theological statements. This witness cannot be highly enough praised and lifted up as an expression of unity in the early church.

Who Are the Poor Today?

What does it mean to "remember the poor"? Who are the poor today? Are you poor? Why are people poor? Does anybody really want to know why this is so? The poor of the world are to be remembered! But they do not ask for our pity. They ask two basic questions: "How are affluence and poverty related in our world today?" and "Are we Christians as a 'family of faith' (6:10) ready to stand up for equality and mutual sharing with the poor?"

We in the rich countries are not told and do not realize how much affluence is built on the back of the world's poor: their cheap labor, their underpaid-for resources, their lack of protection, their lack of power in the world market and political arena. We deceive ourselves if we think we are rich, or at least well off, because we work hard and deserve it. Others work harder and are poorer!

The sentence, "The poor are poor because they are poor," only shows our unwillingness to learn about poverty. To the extent that we are not ready to face the question, we are not ready to "remember the poor."

The story of the rich young man is an example of how Jesus and Paul understand law and gospel in relation to rich and poor (Mk. 10:17–31).

The young man comes to Jesus with the sincere question: "What must I do to inherit eternal life?" Jesus reminds him of the ten commandments, the law of Moses, as his guide. The young man says: "I have been doing it, all of it." In a literal way he has been keeping the law, but this did not fulfill his search for "life," real life, life of eternity, life with integrity, purpose and compassion. Paul would say: The law did not justify him (that is, put his relations with God and others in order). Now Jesus leads him to the test: Is he ready for the self–giving love and sharing of what he has and is, for a life of discipleship? But the young man is not ready. Many of us are not ready. He is not free to follow Jesus; his heart is bound to property, to himself and his belongings. Property in itself is not evil or bad. But it has the power to occupy our hearts, bind our minds to moneymaking, profits, savings and stock maneuverings. But even more important: It prevents us from asking the question: Where does the property come from? Is it just property? What is it for?

Some peasants in Nicaragua once discovered the following while discussing this story: "The rich young man thought he was not stealing, killing, lying—yet he was rich. But God has given the earth to everybody equally. If anybody or any nation has everything the others do not have, they must have stolen it some way. According to the law (and his own consciousness) he had not stolen. Maybe, he inherited it. But he lived from wealth that others were deprived of."

This is very much the painful reality of many Christians in affluent societies. We participate without being conscious, or by being only half conscious of how often this affluence has violated God's commandment to love our neighbor. And we don't know (or we say so) what to do. This is why Jesus implies that only a miracle can save the rich. (See Mk. 10:25–27.) Our relations with many people of the world are not right because of structures of injustice. Human selfishness will not undo it. But with God in our hearts it is possible. Yes, God can convert the hearts of the people in affluent societies. It has happened. Wealth can be shared. Exploitation can be stopped. Justice can come.

And it had better be so because individual wealth and the new creation do not go together. The gift of God's grace wants to express itself in the "fruit of righteousness," our rightly relating to the poor in generous sharing.—*B.W.P.*

The agreement in Jerusalem was a compromise. Christian Jews would continue to live in the tradition of their ancestors, while Gentile Christians would not be forced to adopt the Jewish law. The compromise looked good, as long as the two communities were separate. But as the next incident shows, this compromise did not solve the problems of a growing church in which the Jewish and Gentile Christians had to live together very closely.

Conflict between Church Leaders (2:11–14)

We can assume that there were frequent visits between Antioch and Jerusalem. Cephas (Peter) visited the church in Antioch; we do not know on what occasion. During his visit a strong conflict between him and Paul occurred (2:11). As often in his letters, Paul unravels the story from the end and gives the details as he goes along. This might be due to his dictating the letter.

What had happened? Cephas during his visit in Antioch

22

lived freely with the Gentile Christians, sharing meals, most likely also the eucharistic meal with them. As a religious Jew, he was not supposed to share in this way with the uncircumcised. (Peter says to Cornelius the Roman centurion: "You yourselves know that it is unlawful for a Jew to associate with or visit a Gentile," Acts 10:28).

All went well until "certain people came from James," meaning from Jerusalem. The circumcision faction had agreed that Gentiles need not be circumcised. But they did not consider the Jerusalem agreement to mean that the Jewish Christians had the liberty to eat with the Gentiles. The common table became the central point where the community would break, or make it. The life of the church had to reflect the nature of the gospel; this was Paul's view. If everybody was accepted by Christ, everybody had to be accepted at the common table, without condition. This was encapsulated in the baptismal formula: "There is no longer Jew or Greek, slave or free, male and female, for all of you are one in Christ Jesus" (3:28). There can be no division on racial, social, religious or gender lines, lest the nature of the gospel be betrayed. A similar conflict on social lines had arisen in Corinth around the Lord's Supper (1 Cor. 11:17–34).

Peter had withdrawn from the common meal with the Gentiles in order not to be seen transgressing the ritual laws. Paul bluntly called this an act of "fear of the circumcision faction" (2:12). On theological ground, Peter had no argument for withdrawal. He himself had given an outstanding example of the "freedom in Christ" when he visited the house of the Roman centurion Cornelius after a vision. At that occasion he said: "I truly understand that God shows no partiality, but in every nation anyone who fears him and does what is right is acceptable to him" (Acts 10:35). However, we do not know exactly at what time this event happened in Peter's life. In Antioch, Peter seemed to give in to pressure from his home church in Jerusalem, which upheld the principle of a separate Judaic version of the gospel, and that meant separate tables.

For the church in Antioch this was a terrible blow:

23

Christians could no longer gather at the same table. It was the more serious as Peter pulled others with him, including, for the time, the highly respected Barnabas. Paul called this sheer hypocrisy (2:13). This incident proved that the matter had not really been well thought out at the Jerusalem Council and Peter had fallen back into a conservative position, denying the "freedom of Christ." Therefore Paul challenged Peter in public, maybe in a community meeting, exposing his weak position and contradicting behavior. "Peter stood self–condemned," because he was not "acting consistently with the truth of the gospel" (2:14).

The gospel is contrary to all human–made divisions. With all his rhetorical talent Paul puts it in a poignant sentence: "If you, though a Jew, live like a Gentile and not like a Jew, how can you compel the Gentiles to live like Jews" (2:14)? This means: if you as a Jew can afford, while you are here, to live without keeping the Mosaic law and eat with the Gentiles, how can you behave in a way that makes Gentiles feel they ought to act according to Jewish laws?

We do not hear about Peter's response, nor how the controversy ended in Antioch. Paul wanted to present the story and the argument to the Galatians so that they could draw their own conclusions. Eventually, Paul's wider, all–embracing theological understanding of the gospel became the norm for the church throughout its history. Hence we today do not have to keep the Jewish law. But legalism has remained a danger to the churches' self–understanding. Circumcision was abandoned. The inclusive ritual, baptism, which was equally open to everybody, including women, prevailed.

Doing Theology

Paul, in his letter, does theology by telling his life story. We often think we should not mention personal things when speaking about the Christian faith. But why? Many lay people, especially women, consider theology the field of experts who produce learned discourses on theological topics. But the Greek word "theo–logia" means: speaking of God, communicating God in our lives. Therefore "doing theology" is not the domain of experts only.

The term "doing theology" indicates that we not only "talk" theology, but "do" theology, act, live theology in our daily lives, everyone of us.

A few examples are given here to encourage you to "do" your own theology. You might be surprised how many things are to be discovered.

Letterwriting is an important way of doing theology as we have seen from Paul's letter. For example, my mother in her letters to me, always includes some of her quiet early morning meditations, written at the kitchen table, or some hymns or poems. By this she continues to teach me.

In recent German church history we have read the famous *Letters and Papers from Prison* by Dietrich Bonhoeffer, a German theologian who participated in the conspiracy against Hitler. He wrote from prison the most profound, beautiful and moving witness of faith in our times. Bonhoeffer was later executed by the Nazis.

Witness letters are a special type of letter. People write in order to give witness about an unknown difficult situation in their lives: a sickness, a persecution, an awakening. By their witness they awaken our consciousness and ask for our support. In recent years the churches have received many such letters from Christians in many parts of the world, from Guatemala, from Korea, from South Africa, from China and other places. Do you remember any such letters? Do you have other letters in mind, of a more personal nature?

Storytelling is not a new thing for Christians. Most of Jesus' theology was done by storytelling. We call such stories parables. In a story a simple truth can be told and we read from it easily (or after some reflection) the meaning for our lives. Storytelling can mean: to tell our own stories, to tell folk stories, traditional stories, Biblical stories. Women have always been good story-tellers because they are close to children who learn about life and faith through stories. Western theology has often been criticized for its abstract nature. But at the root of our faith was a storytelling rabbi called Jesus of Nazareth. Some of the great storytellers are, for example, the Minjing theologians in Korea. The famous Russian writer Leo Tolstoy wrote short stories with powerful theological messages. The Jewish phi-losopher Martin Buber has gathered and published many of the stories of the Hassidim, an enthusiastic renewal movement of the eighteenth and nineteenth centuries in Eastern Europe. In the World Council of Churches we once collected, in a small book entitled *By Our Lives*, stories of women from all over the world as they relate to biblical stories. Why don't you begin to tell your own stories?

Poems and Songs are very frequently used in our church life. How much affirmation and teaching can be re-ceived from hymns and gospel songs! A modern hymn writer, Fred Kaan, wrote a poem, which Doreen Potter set to music, that explains Paul's theology in a very easy way:

> Help us accept each other
> as Christ accepted us.
> Teach us, as sisters, brothers,
> each person to embrace.
> Be present Lord among us
> and help us to believe
> we are ourselves accepted
> and meant to love and live.

Communal Reflections/Discussions are used today by many groups to discover the meaning of the Bible and to translate it into the reality they are living. One of the first of this kind was published by Ernesto Cardenal, and called *The Gospel in Solentiname* (Orbis, 1982). Simple peasants and fisherfolk in conversation with one another developed a kind of communal preaching that confirms that God has given to all of us talents and gifts for the building of the community.

Doing Theology by Art and Creative Work includes dance, drama, painting, sculpture, architecture, creative needlework (*e.g.* quiltmaking) and even cooking, flower–arranging and many other things. Artists and writers give contemporary expressions to our faith. The woodcarvings of Aszriah Mbata from South Africa, for example, place the crucifixion of Christ in the middle of a black township in South Africa. Marc Chagall, the famous painter of biblical themes, once wrote about his art: "For me the fulfillment of art and life come from biblical sources. Maybe the people will proclaim again the words of love which I bring back (with my pictures). One day, maybe, there will be no more enemies in this world—and like a mother in travail gives birth to her child, so the young and the not–so–young will create a world of love in a completely new color . . . " (Adapted).—*B.W.P.*

Paul's Theology in a Nutshell (2:15–21)

From here on the letter picks up the theological argument. The actual events in Paul's life serve as evidence to pull the Galatians back from their confusion about "the law" to the "freedom of the gospel." And the theological arguments (chapters 3 and 4) are fully aimed at helping the community live as free persons in Christ (chapters 5 and 6).

Verses 15 and 16 contain Paul's theological position in a nutshell. By birth, Jews considered themselves as the "chosen people," having God's favor by having the Torah, the law. Gentiles were called "sinners" without the law. However, if a Jew would not keep the law, he or she would also be called a "sinner" (2:15). The central message of the life and death of Jesus Christ was that humanity would not gain religious fulfillment, acceptance, human identity and integrity by meticulous implementation of the law, or a wrong or hypocritical use of it. No religious apparatus or obedience to the letter could by itself solve anybody's quest for life.

Justification/righteousness in Jewish thought and language meant right relations with God, with oneself and with one another. This state of justification could be recognized in the complete inner freedom of a person, an unforced and voluntary response with one's whole life to God's goodness. And because God's goodness had expressed itself in the life and death of Jesus Christ, who fulfilled the law and the prophets in his own unique way, he was "the way and the truth and the life" for Jews and Gentiles alike (2:15, 16).

In verse 17 Paul inserts a rhetorical question, as he oftern does, using the rules of Greek rhetoric, which he had obviously learned in his Hellenistic upbringing in Tarsus. If Christ himself had liberated Paul from the burden of the law, could his "free life style" be regarded as "sin"? Then Christ would have to be blamed for promoting this "sin." This argument aims at showing the absurd logic of the position of Paul's opponents. Paul's position was clear: One cannot harmonize Judaistic legalism with freedom in Christ (2:17). Paul cannot go back on what he has been preaching to all Jews and Gentiles. "But if I build up again the very thing that I once tore down, then I demonstrate that I am a transgressor" (2:18).

Paul sees his own life in parallel to Christ's life. His overzealous restless obsession as a Pharisee led to his breakdown on the Damascus road. "Through the law I died to the law." The inner death was an excruciating experience. "I have been crucified with Christ" (2:19), claims Paul, but he also claims that it gave a totally new meaning to his life. It changed his relation to God and to other people. Only after this was he able to live integrally and fulfilled for God's purpose: "so that I might live to God."

In an almost mystical way he sees himself "inhabited" by Christ. Christ fills him out as a person, frees him from the tormenting search for identity, security and religious assurance. Indeed, Christ has taken residence in his very body, in his existence. "It is no longer I who live but it is Christ who lives in me." His earthly existence "in the flesh" is now empowered by a new strength, a new freedom, a new acceptance, which gives him what we all seek—human wholeness. "I live by faith." The self–giving love of God's son enables him to live a free, self–giving life of love (2:20).

"For Me": 2:20

This verse has had a profound effect on many Christians. The reformer Martin Luther lectured on the Letter to the Galatians from 1516 to 1535 when his lectures were published. He wrote: "The Epistle to the Galatians is my epistle; I have betrothed myself to it; it is my wife." When he came to 2:20, he wrote, "mark well the little words 'for me.'" The whole weight of Christ's saving work was on this "for me," and the way each of us responds to it.

On Pentecost Sunday, 21 May 1738, Charles Wesley lay seriously ill in bed. Some friends read to him the comments of Luther on Galatians 2:20. Wesley felt a deep awakening of the presence of Christ in him and soon wrote a hymn:

And can it be that I should gain
An interest in the Savior's blood?
Died he for me who caused his pain?
For me, who him to death pursued?
Amazing love! How can it be
That Thou, my Lord, shouldst die for me?

No condemnation now I dread,
Jesus, with all in him, is mine;
Alone in him, my living head,
And clothed in righteousness divine,
Bold I approach the eternal throne
And claim the crown, through Christ, my own."

Charles Wesley became a leader of the evangelical awakening of the eighteeth century, and its great hymn writer. Many of his hymns evoke these words of Paul in 2:20.—*P.P.*

———————

Again, Paul cannot draw back from his experience, he cannot compromise, because this would mean he would "nullify the grace of God." If the old Pharisaic way of religiosity, "justification through the law," were sufficient; if it had been truly liberating for him, then Christ's life and death would have remained an accidental episode in the history of religion and soon to be forgotten. "Then Christ died for nothing" (2:21).

3. Now That Faith Has Come

3 You foolish Galatians! Who has bewitched you? It was before your eyes that Jesus Christ was publicly exhibited as crucified! [2]The only thing I want to learn from you is this: Did you receive the Spirit by doing the works of the law or by believing what you heard? [3]Are you so foolish? Having started with the Spirit, are you now ending with the flesh? [4]Did you experience so much for nothing?— if it really was for nothing. [5]Well then, does God supply you with the Spirit and work miracles among you by your doing the works of the law, or by your believing what you heard?

6 Just as Abraham "believed God, and it was reckoned to him as righteousness," [7]so, you see, those who believe are the descendants of Abraham. [8]And the scripture, foreseeing that God would justify the Gentiles by faith, declared the gospel beforehand to Abraham, saying, "All the Gentiles shall be blessed in you." [9]For this reason, those who believe are blessed with Abraham who believed.

10 For all who rely on the works of the law are under a curse; for it is written, "Cursed is everyone who does not observe and obey all the things written in the book of the law." [11]Now it is evident that no one is justified before God by the law; for "The one who is righteous will live by faith." [12]But the law does not rest on faith; on the contrary, "Whoever does the works of the law will live by them." [13]Christ redeemed us from the curse of the law by becoming

31

a curse for us—for it is written, "Cursed is everyone who hangs on a tree"— [14]in order that in Christ Jesus the blessing of Abraham might come to the Gentiles, so that we might receive the promise of the Spirit thorugh faith.

15 Brothers and sisters, I give an example from daily life: once a person's will has been ratified, no one adds to it or annuls it. [16]Now the promises were made to Abraham and to his offspring; it does not say, "And to offsprings,: as of many; but it says, "And to your offspring," that is, to one person, who is Christ. [17]My point is this: the law, which came four hundred thirty years later, does not annul a covenant previously ratified by God, so as to nullify the promise. [18]For if the inheritance comes from the law, it no longer comes from the promise; but God granted it to Abraham through the promise.

19 Why then the law? It was added because of transgressions, until the offspring would come to whom the promise had been made; and it was ordained through angels by a mediator. [20]Now a mediator involves more than one party; but God is one.

21 Is the law then opposed to the promises of God? Certainly not! For if a law had been given that could make alive, then righteousness would indeed come through the law.[22] But the scripture has imprisoned all things under the power of sin, so that what was promised through faith in Jesus Christ might be given to those who believe.

23 Now before faith came, we were imprisoned and guarded under the law until faith would be revealed. [24]Therefore the law was our disciplinarian until Christ came, so that we might be justified by faith. [25]But now that faith has come, we are no longer subject to a disciplinarian, [26]for in Christ

Jesus you are all children of God through faith. many of you as were baptized into Christ have clothed yourselves with Christ. ²⁸There is no longer Jew or Greek, there is no longer slave or free, there is no longer male and female; for all of you are one in Christ Jesus. ²⁹And if you belong to Christ, then you are Abraham's offspring, heirs according to the promise.

In the first two chapters, Paul has been affirming his experience of Christ and his call as an apostle. He ends by asserting: "I do not nullify the grace of God; for if justification/righteousness comes through the law, then Christ died for nothing" (2:21). For Paul, the central reality for us is God's grace—God's free self–giving love, revealed in Christ crucified as our redeemer. This is the message Paul preached to the Galatians. It is the character of this message that Paul seeks to articulate in the next two chapters.

You Foolish Galatians! (3:1–5)

Paul begins by reminding the Galatians of the gospel message in a very forceful manner: "You foolish Galatians! Who has bewitched you? It was before your eyes that Jesus Christ was publicly exhibited as crucified!" How bold to call the Galatians foolish! The word does not mean intellectually stupid, or ignorant. It means lacking discernment about the very foundation of the faith they had embraced.

Jesus had used the same word when addressing the two apostles whom he encountered on their way to Emmaus. They recounted what they had heard and experienced in Jerusalem about Jesus of Nazareth. Jesus exclaimed: "Oh how foolish you are, and how slow of heart to believe all that the prophets have declared! Was it not necessary that the Messiah should suffer these things and then enter into his glory?" Then Luke adds: "Beginning with Moses and all the prophets, he interpreted to them the things about himself in all the scriptures" (Lk. 24:25–27).

This is exactly what Paul is about to do. When he passionately writes, "you foolish Galatians," he is pointing to their failure to connect the preaching they had heard to the promises of the scriptures. They were "bewitched," dazzled by another teaching. They could no longer discern, grasp and rely on the true nature of their faith and its consequences. Paul asks bluntly: "Did you receive the Spirit by the works of the law or by believing what you heard"? When they heard and accepted the gospel they felt the power of God in the Spirit. The real miracle they had experienced was their ready acceptance of this new faith. It had transformed their relationships. It had led to the building up of communities of believers. It had freed them from their pagan past and given them a new outlook on life.

Was all this for nothing? How was it possible for them to imagine that they must now add the practice of the law? Was this not relapsing from the high point of life in the Spirit to a struggle with the "flesh," that is, their own unaided efforts?

The Promise to Abraham (3:6–9)

Paul is now forced to appeal to scripture as he challenges the Galatians. Those preachers and teachers who were exhorting them to embrace another way were also appealing to scripture. Paul goes beyond the law of Moses to the call of Abraham and to the promise made to him. This call by God came as a new beginning in the human story. Genesis 1–11 describes creation, the fall of Adam and Eve, and all that followed, down to the story of the Tower of Babel when God scattered the people abroad over the face of the earth (Gen. 11:9). God now calls Abraham, who was a pagan, as the Galatians had been: "Go from your country and your kindred and your father's house to a land that I will show you. I will make of you a great nation, and I will bless you, and make your name great, so that you will be a blessing . . . and in you all the families of the earth shall be blessed" (Gen. 12:1–3). And the scripture says: Abraham "believed the LORD; and the LORD reckoned it to him as righteousness" (Gen. 15:6). Thus, says Paul, all persons who have faith are in fact blessed as they share Abraham's faith.

What does all this mean? There are three words here that need to be explained in order to get their proper significance. They are "righteousness," "blessing," and "faith." They are central to what Paul is saying to the Galatians and to us in this letter. They are familiar words. But their very familiarity has become strange to us. Though our earliest copies of Paul's letter are in Greek, he no doubt also had the Hebrew meanings in mind as he wrote.

"Righteousness/justification" as used in Galatians means right relationship. This is not a legal or business concept. It represents a reality that is concerned with how people relate to each other. Relationships are basic to our human existence. Living means relating to one another. Relationship is a covenant word—the bond between persons for a common purpose. The word "justification" is a substitute for "righteousness." "Justification" is the Latin expression, *justitia*. The root of the word is from the old Indo–European "*ju*," to bind.) Justification/justice signified being bound to God and one another in mutual commitment. The righteousness of God is the inner character of God who relates to people and creation by binding them together in right relationship to one another. This speaks of a God who seeks to fill people and things with integrity and the capacity to become and be what they were destined to be, as made in God's image.

God manifests righteousness by blessing. The word "bless" means to share one's power, one's strength, one's life with another, to be with the other. God blesses Abraham by "accompanying" him with divine power, enabling Abraham to live and find his pilgrim way, filled with the promise of

God. We too say "bless you" to one another. It is an instinctive way of affirming our solidarity with the other, and wishing the other well.

But to receive the blessing, one must be reckoned righteous, put in the way of right relationship. To be in that way is to have faith. Faith in Hebrew is *emunah*, from the verb *aman*, from which we get the well–known affirmation, *Amen*. It means not only faith, but faithfulness, trust, trustfulness, trustworthiness, confidence, reliability, commitment. It is also the word for "truth"—what is to be believed, what is worthy of trust, what is reliable and evokes our commitment. For Paul, this faith is the gift of God, a work of grace, and also the act by which we respond and relate to the righteous, faithful God who has come and comes to us. This God calls us to believe, trust and rely on the divine promises. We are called to live in faithfulness to God. This was what Abraham did. He had faith in God, and this faith was manifested in his being righteous and blessed. We who have faith participate in the life of righteousness and in the blessing of God.

Christ Redeems Us (3:10–14)

What was being offered to the Galatians, however, by the intruding preachers and teachers, was a way of life that relied on the law as the means of becoming righteous before God. Paul, writing from the knowledge of his own experience, is conscious that there is no future, or way through, on this course. Paul reminds the Galatians of a word from Deuteronomy 27:26: "Cursed be anyone who does not uphold the words of this law by observing them." It is a law that included 613 prescriptions and prohibitions. It kept people in a constant frenzy of meritorious self–effort. The word "curse" means the condition of being cut off from relationship, a condition that leads to doom and spiritual death. Cursed is the opposite of being blessed. Since no one can fully carry out all that the law demands, no one can become righteous. No one can have right, direct relations with God.

Paul is convinced with the Psalmist that "no one living is righteous before you [God]." (Ps. 143:2, quoted in Gal. 2:16.) Paul rather turns to the word of the prophet Habakkuk: "The righteous live by their faith" (Hab. 2:4). This word is uttered in the context of the prophet's cry to God to come to the rescue of the people of Israel, and punish the leaders who are oppressing them. Destruction and violence are everywhere: "The law becomes slack, and justice never prevails" (1:2–4). The Babylonians are permitted to come to check the tyranny of the rulers of Judah. They quickly come in their fury as a force of judgment, for "your eyes are too pure to behold evil, and you cannot look on wrongdoing" (1:13). But the Babylonians are far too cruel in their punishment. So the prophet prays to God and pleads for his people. And God says:

Write the vision;
    make it plain on tablets,
    so that a runner may read it.
For there is still a vision for the appointed time;
    it speaks of the end, and does not lie.
If it seems to tarry, wait for it;
    it will surely come, it will not delay.
Look at the proud!
    Their spirit is not right in them,
    but the righteous live by their faith.
                                        (Hab. 2:2–4).

The prophet had seen clearly that those responsible for carrying out the law had slacked in their duty and were puffed up. They had acted unjustly toward their people. This was the way of death. Only those who were righteous, who had right relations with God and with the people, in just dealings, would live.

Law is not enough, for those who practice it forget the lawgiver's demand that law is for justice and righteousness.

Faith that relies on the God of the covenant lives in and practices righteousness.

What Paul is trying to tell the Galatians is that, after having accepted the message of salvation in Christ by faith, to now accept circumcision would oblige them to obey the whole law, which they could not do. This would utterly frustrate and defeat them because there is no way to righteousness by doing the whole law. The law does say: "Whoever does the works of the law will live by them (Lev. 18:5). But what comes about is really the curse, the awareness of doom, "no exit." This is the blind alley in which the people of the old covenant found themselves. This is the blind alley that Paul encountered when he experienced Christ on the road to Damascus. It was the moment of illumination when a new path was opened for him. What was this new light that dawned on Paul?

Paul answers with his great declaration of faith: "Christ redeemed us from the curse of the law by becoming a curse for us—for it is written, 'Cursed is everyone who hangs on a tree' (Gal. 3:13)." The law decrees that everyone who is condemned to death by hanging on a tree is cursed (Deut. 21:22–23). Well, Christ was hung and died on a tree, the cross (Acts 5:30; 10:39). He thus became a curse. But what <u>he did was for us.</u> Jews and Gentiles alike. God was in Christ where we have been and are in our broken human condition. Christ is in complete solidarity with us. He made our doom his own. Hanging from the cross he died our death. Through his death he redeems us, "buys us out or back." Paul is using a metaphor from the world of slavery. Cursed meant being cast off, cast out. A person who was cast out by the family or tribe ended up a slave. To redeem the slave is to buy out and therefore liberate the slave. The freed slave can then be incorporated in renewed relationship with the community. He/she is considered righteous, reconnected, sharing the blessing as God's free person.

All through this letter Paul again and again declares Christ's liberating work "for us" and "for our sins" (1:4; 2:20; 3:13: 4:4–5; 6:14). In other letters he speaks in the same terms. For example, he writes to the Romans: "God shows his love for us in that while we were yet sinners Christ died for us" (5:8; see also 1 Cor. 15:3; 2 Cor. 5:21). It is the immensity of God's grace—God's free self-giving love—that is revealed in what Christ did to free us. This, says Paul, has made the promise to Abraham a reality. The blessing is now present in and among us through the power of the Spirit. This blessing is for all, both Jews and Gentiles, who freely respond to it by faith.

Our Methodist Heritage

It is important, at this point, to recall our Methodist heritage. Reference has already been made to Paul's influence on Charles Wesley in Galatians 2:20, through Martin Luther's comment. On 24 May, 1738, John Wesley went to a meeting place in London where someone was reading from Martin Luther's Commentary on Romans. It was on chapter 1, verses 16–17: "For I am not ashamed of the gospel: it is the power of God for salvation to every one who has faith, to the Jew first and also to the Greek. For in it the righteousness of God has been revealed through faith for faith; as it is written: 'The one who is righteous shall live by faith.'"

Paul quotes from the prophecy of Habakkuk in Galatians 3:11, as he does in Romans. It was Luther's emphasis on faith as a living commitment to Christ that led Wesley to feel the liberating power of God in his life. He had the sense of assurance that he was a child of God. He rushed to see his brother Charles in his sick bed, and declared: "I believe." Charles told him of his heartwarming experience three days before. He had composed a hymn, which they started to sing together:

39

Where shall my wondering soul begin?
How shall I all to heaven aspire?
A slave redeemed from death and sin,
A brand plucked from eternal fire,
How shall I equal triumphs raise,
And sing my great deliverer's praise?

It took nearly ten months of prayer and reflection for John Wesley to answer those questions. In late March 1739, Wesley received an urgent call from his friend, George Whitefield, the famous evangelical preacher in England and America. It was to come to Bristol—a city where the slave trade of blacks and whites was flourishing; where there was great poverty in the midst of wealth; where there was a notorious prison in which people were hung for small offenses; where most of the people were hardly touched by the gospel. Wesley arrived at the end of the month. On the Sunday following his arrival, he preached in a church on the Sermon on the Mount. The next day, 2 April, 1739, Wesley wrote that he decided to become more vile by preaching in the open air to some three thousand people. He chose his text carefully. It was from Luke's Gospel: "The Spirit of the Lord is upon me, because he has anointed me to preach good news to the poor, he has sent me to proclaim release to the captives and recovering of sight to the blind, to set at liberty those who are oppressed, to proclaim the acceptable year of the Lord" (4:18–19).

This message of freedom in Christ was the beginning of the Methodist Movement 250 years ago. Wesley said that "Methodism was raised up by God to reform the nation and especially the Church, and to spread Scriptural Holiness throughout the world." Wesley saw scriptural holiness as a life devoted to God and persons everywhere in liberating love.—*P.P.*

Why the Law? (3:15–24)

Paul takes up the claims of those opponents who have come to disturb the Galatians. For them the gospel of redemption in Christ is not enough. The Galatians are therefore being pressed to adhere to the law of Moses. Paul has two comments to make.

The first is to a well–known legal custom in the Roman Empire. When a man dies, his will is ratified. (In Roman times only men could make a will, and the inheritance was designated to men only.) Nothing could be added to the will. "Will" also means "testament" or "covenant" as in verse 17. The true will, testament or covenant was given by Abraham to whom God said: "by your offspring shall all the nations of the earth gain blessing for themselves, because you have obeyed my voice" (Gen. 22:18). This word was spoken after Abraham tried obediently to offer his son Isaac as a sacrifice, even though Isaac was the only living guarantee of the promise of the blessing to all nations (Gen. 22:1–17). Paul is asserting that it is Christ who fulfilled the promise contained in Isaac. He made possible and available this new relationship, this righteousness, this blessing for the Gentiles.

Paul is not the only New Testament witness to the fulfillment of the promise of Abraham in Jesus Christ. Matthew's Gospel begins with the words: "An account of the genealogy of Jesus the Messiah, the son of David, the son of Abraham . . . " (Mt. 1:1). "Son of David" represents the promise of the Messiah, Christ. "Son of Abraham" represents the universal promise of the blessing to all nations. The Gospel ends with the commission of Jesus to his disciples: "Go therefore and make disciples of all nations . . . and remember, I am with you always, to the end of the age" (Mt. 28:18–20). When John the Baptist comes to the Jews with his call to repentance and renewal, he says to them: "Bear fruit worthy of repentance. Do not presume to say to yourselves, 'We have Abraham as our ancestor'; for I tell you, God is able from these stones to raise up children to

Abraham." And John goes on to announce the coming of Jesus in the power of the Spirit (Mt. 3:8–11).

In Luke's Gospel, Mary sings a song of praise and prophecy as the baby Jesus stirs in her womb. Her song, now referred to as the Magnificat, concludes its assurance of righteousness, with the words: "according to the promise [God] made to our ancestors, to Abraham and to his descendants forever" (Lk. 1:55).

When Zacchaeus, the rich tax collector, promises to put right the wrongs he has done to the people and to re–establish more trustful relations, Jesus says to him: "Today salvation has come to this house, because he too is a son of Abraham" (Lk. 19:9).

In John's Gospel Jesus has a controversy with the Jewish leaders who claim to be the descendants of Abraham and therefore of his heritage. Jesus tells them: "Whoever is from God hears the words of God. The reason you do not hear them is that you are not from God." He ends his debate with them by saying: " . . . before Abraham was, I am" (Jn. 8:33, 47, 58).

Paul's second comment to the Galatians about those who want to give chief place to the Mosaic law is that this law came 430 years after the promise given and the covenant made with Abraham. The covenant with Abraham, therefore, takes precedence over the Mosaic law and has a wider reference than the people of Israel. The promise is to all the nations. It is this promise made alive in Christ the liberator.

What then was the function of the law? Why would the Christian Jews press it so hard on the Galatians? This is a tricky question for Paul. In his letter to the Romans, written after this letter to the Galatians, Paul says: " . . . the law is holy, and the commandment is holy and just and good" (Rom. 7:12). In an autobiographical letter to the Philippians, Paul confesses: "Circumcised on the eighth day, a member of the people of Israel, of the tribe of Benjamin, a Hebrew born of Hebrews; as to the law, a Phrarisee; as to zeal a persecutor of the church; as to righteousness under the law, blameless. Yet, whatever gains I had, these I have come to regard as loss because of Christ . . . found in him, not having a righteousness of my own, that comes from the law, but one that comes through faith in Christ, the righteousness from God based on faith" (Phil. 3:5–7,9).

Paul, therefore, approaches this question of the function of the law with both respect for the law and an acute sense of its limitations, based on his own experience and observation.

First, Paul seems to say in verses 19–22 that the law, by its very existence, draws attention to our evil inclinations. People tend to do what they are forbidden. There is a sense in which the negative way in which the ten commandments are given points to the difficulty of maintaining them: "You shall not . . . " (Ex. 20:1–17). Paul himself knew the dilemma: "I delight in the law of God, in my inmost self, but I see in my members another law at war with the law of my mind, making me captive to the law of sin that dwells in my members. Wretched man that I am! Who will rescue me from this body of death? Thanks be to God through Jesus Christ our Lord! So then, with my mind I am a slave to the law of God, but with my flesh I am a slave to the law of sin" (Rom. 7:22–25). Paul therefore sees the law functioning to make us reveal the full extent of our rebellion against God. However, in whatever manner the law came to humanity, we are dealing with one God who has provided in Jesus Christ the way in which the law is fulfilled by our faith relationship to him.

Second, Paul asserts that a function of the law is to keep us in check, to hold us back from falling into anarchy. This is done by a custodian till we come of age. In the Greek/ Roman world, a custodian, *paidagogus*, was a slave who was given the responsibility of looking after a school boy before his puberty. (Girls were considered as private persons and had no right of citizenship or inheritance.) The slave accompanied the boy to school and back. He saw to it that he did not run away. He made sure that the boy had all the materials necessary for school, and that he did not get into trouble. He even had the right to punish the boy. These custodians had a bad reputation for being severe. But they were often respected. The law, then, had this task as a custodian "until faith was revealed," "until Christ came." "Now that faith has come" this task can cease.

Law, Legalism, Freedom in Christ

If we speak today about the law, we do not think like Paul of the Mosaic law. People think more of other things like, "Buckle up, it's the law." "Law" is for most people the legislation of our countries that protects our private and public life. If legislation is just and democratic, then the law is a positive force. To come in conflict with the law means to do something that harms others. The Mosaic law has this positive intention; in addition, it goes much further. It does protect the community from grave offenses (do not kill, steal, lie, etc.), but it also gives instructions on health, marriage, property. And all is grounded in the relation to God. Therefore the law puts life in the context of worship and divine revelation. When the law was given, people had the choice between blessing and curse (Deut. 30:19–20); because the law was meant to enable life in the community as well as to enhance the proper relation to God. We know that Jesus and Paul (and the prophets) attacked a deteriorated practice of the law. "Law" had become a tyranny and a rigid straightjacket. In many stories, Jesus tackled the superficial and perverted religious practice of the Scribes and Pharisees. He had given the whole law and the prophets a new meaning, turning it from outside observance into the "law written in our hearts," which he fulfilled up to his death.

Since we are not really tempted "to fall back into the Mosaic law," it is not easy to see what Paul's attack against the "law" means for us today. And yet, it is not just the "law" as a certain body of religious instruction that Paul attacks. It is a whole way of life; a life that clings to rules and regulations instead of taking responsibility for one's self and for each other; that lives rather by "law and order" than by human and divine considerations for the life of the community.

In the history of my German people we have had a drastic experience of how the obedience to the given law was the source of major tragedy for humanity. Under the Nazi regime of Hitler, the majority of Germans considered obedience to the law, and to the political leaders who made them, a great virtue. They stopped asking whether their obedience was human or responsible. The most awful things were done conscientiously because obedience to the given law and instructions was more important than one's own responsibility or human feelings. Many expected to "save their life," to find ultimate fulfillment by this blind obedience, having put all their trust in the system that promised to restore German nationhood, but meanwhile destroyed the lives of millions of people. When asked, afterwards, why they did what they did in Auschwitz, persons often answered, "We only did our duty."

There were not many Germans at the time to break out of this rigid legalism of Nazism. It is an extreme example, but it teaches us something.

Today there are many written and unwritten laws surrounding us that promise us life: happiness, success, excitement. To make it to the top, to be successful, to earn lots of money, to experience great excitement, these are the promises of consumer societies. Our culture, our family tradition, our society provide us with a lot of "laws." Many churches present their orders and services as sacred and do not allow for questioning. New sects promise ultimate fulfillment at the cost of strict obedience.

What does "freedom in Christ" mean in such situations?

In Christ's self–giving love, all attempts at self–redemption, all obedience to fashionable laws and authorities are shown for what they are: means of leading people astray. "In Christ" we have become mature, are not anymore children who must be told: do this, do that. But we know the "law of Christ" in our hearts and consciences. We teach it through community service and through our worship. It guides us like a red thread through the uncertainties of life. We often do not have clear–cut answers for everything, but we have the "law of Christ" to help us live as free people, responsible to each other and ultimately to God.

—B.W.P.

Breaking Down Barriers (3:25–29)

Paul understood the history of God's salvation of broken humanity to have gone through three stages: (1) The call of Abraham, his response of faith and the promise that through him the nations of the world would be blessed; (2) the law and covenant given through Moses to the people of Israel acting as custodian and preparing the way for (3) the coming of Christ who, by his redeeming work, frees us to become by faith what we were created to be—children of God.

This liberating event is celebrated by baptism. No one knows for sure what the mode of baptism was in Paul's time, but it has been assumed that at least at times, it was by immersion. We are aware of baptismal facilities for immersion very early in the life of the church and some have speculated that the new believers put off their old clothes and plunged into the water as a symbol of their participating in Christ's crucifixion and death. They then rose from the water with the risen Christ and put on new clothes. That was the symbol of "putting on Christ" (3:27; also Col. 3:5–11). It is significant that the first record of Jesus' preaching, which took place at Nazareth, places his sermon in the context of Isaiah 61:1–2, announcing good news to the poor, release to the captives, sight to the blind, liberty to the oppressed (Lk. 4:18–21). The prophet Isaiah goes on to record the response of the people to this liberating word:

> I will greatly rejoice in the LORD,
>   my whole being shall exult in my God;
> for [God] has clothed me with the garments of salvation,
>   [God] has covered me with the robe of righteousness.
>   (Is. 61:10)

Paul's symbol of "putting on Christ" is reminiscent of Isaiah's language of putting on "garments of salvation" and "the robe of righteousness." Paul continues to describe his own experience by saying, "I have been crucified with Christ; and it is no longer I who live but it is Christ who lives in me. And the life I now live in the flesh I live by faith in the Son of God, who loved me and gave himself for me" (2:19b–20). This was such a radically new reality for Paul that, in his final personal note to the Galatians, he calls it "a new creation"(6:15). Something of an entirely different order from what existed before has come into being. And it has profound consequences.

Our right relations (righteousness) with God call for right relations with others at the fundamental levels where we have become divided as human beings. "There is no longer Jew or Greek, there is no longer slave or free, there is no longer male and female; for all of you are one in Christ Jesus" (3:28). How could someone so steeped in the prejudice of his history, religion, and culture rise above it and make such a clear declaration? Paul himself would say it was because of his faith in Christ who fulfilled the promise made to Abraham that all the nations of the earth would be blessed. Paul's dramatic faith and his combative theological reflections had forced him to reach this conclusion. And this declaration can never be contested by anyone who shares the same faith relationship to Christ. For Paul, righteousness/justification by faith means, at the same time, righteousness/justice for all and in all relationships.

The climate in which Paul wrote these words to the Galatians did not permit such noble convictions. For the Jews, there was a gulf fixed between Jew and Gentile, marked particularly by circumcision—a circumcision that certain Jewish converts to Christianity wanted to impose on the Gentile Christians of Galatia. And slavery was an established custom in Israel; though it can be said that, of nearly all the peoples of that time and place, the Jews were probably the most humane in dealing with slaves. They were constantly reminded that they themselves had been liberated by God from slavery in Egypt. Again, at least in their scriptures, the Jews proclaimed that God had created humanity (Adam) as "male and female," both representing the image of God (Gen. 1:27). Indeed, there were two rabbis, Akiba and Simlai, who used to say: "Neither man without woman, nor woman without man, nor both without the *Shekinah*." The "*Shekinah*" means God present, dwelling with us in righteousness. The sense of this rabbinic saying is that male and female find their true being and togetherness, their freedom for each other, in their freedom before and for God, the *Shekinah*. However, in the earliest existing collection of Jewish prayers of thanksgiving (around C.E.* 150), there is a morning prayer in which a male Jew thanks God that he is not made a Gentile, a slave or a woman.

Paul grew up in this tradition. And the irrefutable symbol of female exclusion from the leading functions in Judaism was precisely circumcision. Paul insists that circumcision is not necessary for salvation; and at least in some of his

---

*(C.E., meaning Common Era, is the more universal term for designating time after the birth of Jesus. It is synonymous, in reference to time, with the Christian term, A.D., *Anno Domini*, meaning the Year of Our Lord.)

statements, he affirms women as equal partners with men in God's image and likeness. In his well known confession to the Galatians (3:28), he quotes the phrase "male and female" direct from Genesis 1:27. It is this central faith understanding that must also be used in criticism of Paul himself in such passages as 1 Corinthians 11:2–16—a passage which was written for a particular situation at a particular time, but which has been used by the church as though it had eternal validity.

In the Greek/Roman world the situation was also far from ideal. It is recorded that an early Greek philosopher, Thales (sixth century B.C.), declared that there were three things for which he was grateful to fortune—that he was born a human being and not a beast, a man and not a woman, a Greek and not a barbarian. A barbarian was anyone of whatever race or culture who could not speak Greek and was therefore regarded as uncivilized. The Greek citizen looked down on other peoples. Only the Jews were allowed to carry on their religious practices and be exempt from the imperial worship and the games. Paul has all this in mind when he writes to the Colossians about the new nature that the believer in "Christ crucified and risen" must put on: "In that renewal there is no longer Greek and Jew, circumcised and uncircumcised, barbarian, Scythian, slave and free; but Christ is all and in all!" (Col. 3:11).

When we look around us at the nations and cultures of the world today, we find varying degrees and forms of race, class and sex discrimination and oppression. Indeed, at the Sixth Assembly of the World Council of Churches in Vancouver, 1983, it was stated:

The interlinkages among various manifestations of injustice and oppression are becoming more and more clear. Racism, sexism, class domination, the denial of peoples' rights, caste oppression are all woven together, like a spider's web. Singly and together they are at the root of many injustices which cause much suffering and death. The instruments of oppression which maintain and sustain this web vary from the subtle smile of denial to mammoth military machines.[3]

It is estimated that about 80 percent of the Greco–Roman population were slaves or people without rights as citizens. They were classed as property (*res*, thing, in Latin) and as such had no public standing. It is curious and instructive to reflect that Western countries have boasted of the Greek roots of their democratic constitutions. The Greek ideas and institutions looked democratic, but the levels of participation were depressingly low. Surely the nature, character, and credibility of an institution depend on the level and extent of the participation of those for whom it exists, and who carry its burdens.

Web of Oppression

In one of our women's conferences about global and local solidarity, the participants ran into a major problem. Different groups wanted to gain the attention of the plenary and speak about their issue. They began to compete with each other: Anti–apartheid groups, Philippine solidarity workers, feminist theologians, migrant women workers and several others pressed for time and began to complain about manipulation and domination of the agenda. The meeting was in quite some disarray.

At this point, one of the groups offered a little drama to help resolve the issue. They invited representatives of the different groups to come on the stage and they gave them some instructions. The women stood in their little groups and waited for what was going to happen. Suddenly a strange "animal" moved

on the stage. It was covered with brown blankets, and many legs could be seen underneath, like a centipede. The monster moved slowly towards the women and suddenly raised its head: a big sign was attached to its mouth, reading: SEXISM. Some of the women from one group began to fight the monster by hitting it with paper on its head. But as soon as the monster withdrew its head, another head arose from under the blanket, carrying another sign: RACISM. Other women began to beat the head down only to see a third head emerge: CLASSISM. Several more heads emerged: MILITA-RISM, COLONIALISM, etc. At some point all the women's groups, who so far had battled separately with the different heads of the beast, joined their forces, got at the beast from different sides in a united effort. They managed to put a rope around the whole beast. It dropped all its signs. Triumphantly the women led the tamed monster out of the room.

The message was clear: In today's world, the forces of evil have many different manifestations. It was not until late in the nineteenth century that slavery was abolished in the United States. Later the struggle against racism began, with the churches joining in. This struggle still continues—in fact the monster raises its racism head in renewed strength in many places. The class divisions of our societies are often formed along racial lines. Immigrants to this country experience a level of hostility stronger than ever before.

When Paul put forward his "Magna Charta" of Christian faith (3:28), he implicitly understood the interconnectedness of the issues of injustice and evil. In Christ we cannot be against racism and continue to be sexist. Nor can we fight sexism without recognizing the plight of the poor and deprived. Nobody can be free who does not struggle for the liberation of others. Freedom is for freeing.

In the ecumenical movement we have spoken about

the "web of oppression" of racism, sexism, classism. This web is closely interwoven and holds firm as long as we allow all its manifestations to grow unchallenged. The distortion of the community can only be remedied by restoring right relationships within the community. A concrete involvement to restore justice, and right relationships, is a response to God's righteous acts. The theological interconnectedness of our relation to God and to others proves here its strength and viability.—*B.W.P.*

Paul, a "de Facto" Ally

A contemporary theologian, Susanne Heine, observes: "In feminist literature, Paul is . . . clearly the most attacked person in the New Testament: he has been made responsible for all the misfortunes of a Christian tradition which is hostile to women. Does a reading of Pauline texts confirm the justification of such hatred, or is this not rather the result of questionable exegesis of Paul in schools and from the pulpit?"[4]

There is no doubt that in Paul's letters some things are said that have served to oppress women. In accounts like 1 Corinthians 11:2–16, Paul does not break away from the pattern of the ancient world regarding women.

However, two thousand years of exclusively male interpretation have given these texts a prominence they do not deserve in Paul's thinking and have turned Paul's advice to the Corinthians into a new "law" of male privilege in the church. Such interpretation is more interested in the "letter" of Paul's writing than in the "spirit" of his gospel as expressed in 3:28: "There is no longer Jew or Greek, slave or free, male and female; for you are all one in Christ Jesus."

This Pauline formula goes beyond Hebrew, Greek

and Roman thinking of Paul's time, which ignored or sanctioned slave–holding and women's oppression. In fact, Paul's statement goes even further than the slogan of the French Revolution: "Liberty, Equality, Fraternity (1789)." The French Revolution did not even verbally give equal rights to women. The American Constitution (1787) gave voting (therefore, "equal") rights explicitly only to white, property owning males. (Blacks, Indians, the poor and women were excluded.) Although the churches do not often follow the intention of Paul's revolutionary vision—they rather evade it by spiritualizing it—it is clear that Paul announced freedom for slaves, equality for women, and basic human solidarity among people of different cultures and races, and this through Christ.

Patriarchal legalism has taken 1 Corinthians 11 out of context and built a male hierarchical order on it. Such legalism is not faithful to Paul's conviction that "the written code kills, but the spirit gives life" (2 Cor. 3:6).

There are a few central points where Paul fights tooth and nail for the gospel. One of them is in relation to circumcision. This rite, as said before, was aimed at male believers only. By this very fact it inhibited equality of women and men in the faith community, even if it were not intentional. Paul's concern was that the gospel was open to everybody; that it tore down barriers human beings had erected. Even though he was not explicitly fighting for women's rights, the very fact that he abandoned circumcision as a requirement for Christian males makes him a "de facto" ally for future equality struggles. Baptism, practiced in the Jewish community, but not as a central symbol, became the Christian initiation rite. It was a much more feminine ritual: a "rebirth" in water, indiscriminately including everybody who sought it.

The abolition of circumcision has more often been seen as an odd event in the life of the early church. The women's movement has not discovered as yet the crucial egalitarian principle in it. (And as today Jewish women and men are introducing some blessing ceremonies for newborn girls, this possibly reflects their awareness of the exclusivity of the circumcision ritual.) The Christian women's movement can draw strength and argument from Paul's fight against circumcision and discover him as an ally, even if other statements do not express this. We do not have to swallow the box that contains the medicine. The "box" is Paul's contemporary advise. The "medicine" is Paul's theological breakthrough, his great vision for Christianity as expressed in 3:28.

Paul provides women with a strong basis for criticizing Paul himself. He would be the first to admit that the church has turned his advice to the Corinthians into a new "law" that inhibits the growth and the maturity of the community aimed at in 3:28. Now that women are assuming full spiritual leadership in the churches, many blessings are coming to the communities. Who can deny this? Paul acknowledged in many places the leadership women brought to the early church (*e.g.* Rom. 16:1–16).

It has taken humanity many centuries to condemn and abandon slavery. Racial, ethnic and cultural equality are still fought for. So it is with equality of the sexes. But we cannot live with a vision like 3:28, portraying the future Christian community, without being inspired by it. Only as we strive for a truly inclusive community will we claim the gospel for real.—*B.W.P.*

4. Coming of Age

Galatians

4 My point is this: heirs, as long as they are minors, are no better than slaves, though they are the owners of all the property; ²but they remain under guardians and trustees until the date set by the father. ³So with us; while we were minors, we were enslaved to the elemental spirits of the world. ⁴But when the fullness of time had come, God sent his Son, born of a woman, born under the law, ⁵in order to redeem those who were under the law, so that we might receive adoption as children. ⁶And because you are children, God has sent the Spirit of his Son into our hearts, crying, "Abba! Father!" ⁷So you are no longer a slave but a child, and if a child then also an heir, through God.

8 Formerly, when you did not know God, you were enslaved to beings that by nature are not gods. ⁹Now, however, that you have come to know God, or rather to be known by God, how can you turn back again to the weak and beggarly elemental spirits? How can you want to be enslaved to them again? ¹⁰You are observing special days, and months, and seasons, and years. ¹¹I am afraid that my work for you may have been wasted.

12 Friends, I beg you, become as I am, for I also have become as you are. You have done me no wrong. ¹³You know that it was because of a physical infirmity that I first announced the gospel to you; ¹⁴though my condition put you to the test, you did

not scorn or despise me, but welcomed me as an angel of God, as Christ Jesus. [15]What has become of the good will you felt? For I testify that, had it been possible, you would have torn out your eyes and given them to me. [16]Have I now become your enemy by telling you the truth? [17]They make much of you, but for no good purpose; they want to exclude you, so that you may make much of them. [18]It is good to be made much of for a good purpose at all times, and not only when I am present with you. [19]My little children, for whom I am again in the pain of childbirth until Christ is formed in you, [20]I wish I were present with you now and could change my tone, for I am perplexed about you.

21 Tell me, you who desire to be subject to the law, will you not listen to the law? [22]For it is written that Abraham had two sons, one by a slave woman and the other by a free woman. [23]One, the child of the slave, was born according to the flesh; the other, the child of the free woman, was born through the promise. [24]Now this is an allegory: these women are two covenants. One woman, in fact, is Hagar, from Mount Sinai, bearing children for slavery. [25]Now Hagar is Mount Sinai in Arabia and corresponds to the present Jerusalem, for she is in slavery with her children. [26]But the other woman corresponds to the Jerusalem above; she is free, and she is our mother. [27]For it is written,

"Rejoice, you childless one, you who bear no children,
    burst into song and shout, you who endure no birthpangs;
for the children of the desolate woman are more numerous
    than the children of the one who is married."
[28]Now you, my friends, are children of the promise, like Isaac. [29]But just as at that time the child who was

born according to the flesh persecuted the child who was born according to the Spirit, so it is now also. [30]But what does the scripture say? "Drive out the slave and her child; for the child of the slave will not share the inheritance with the child of the free woman." So then, friends, we are children, not of the slave but of the free woman.

Paul has not finished his theological struggle with the Galatians. He is especially concerned about the people who are trying to persuade them to have an understanding of the Christian faith different from the one he had proclaimed. There is more that he wants to tell the Galatians because there is more at stake in this conflict.

Under Guardians and Powers (4:1–3, 8–11)

Paul reintroduces the example of the child who has not reached the age of responsibility, an age the father will determine (3:23–24). The child's condition is practically that of a slave. Even though legally lord of the father's inheritance (4:1–2), the minor has no right of decision. Decisions are in fact taken for the child by appointed guardians and trustees, who control both person and property. Paul is here referring to the Roman law of "guardianship for a minor"—a law with which the Galatians would be familiar. The guardian looked after the minor's person and movements. The trustee was responsible for managing the property.

What Paul wants to draw from this example in Roman custom is that humanity, Jew and Gentile alike, has not come of age by some natural process. The minority status of the Jews was through the Mosaic law, which acted as guardian and trustee until Christ came. There was, in Roman law, a day set by the father when the minor would be declared as coming of age and as entering into responsible existence. So it is the free decision of God to send the son to liberate us to come of age as free responsible persons.

Paul now turns to the Galatians themselves and reminds them of their minority status as Gentile pagans. When he came to them to proclaim the gospel of Christ crucified, he was aware of the similarity of their position to his former situation as a Jew under the law. That is why he says: "So with us: while we were minors, we were enslaved to the elemental spirits of the world" (4:3). What does this phrase mean?

The word Paul uses for "elemental spirits" is *stoicheia*. There was no word like that in the language of the Jews, so it is not found in the Greek Old Testament. But it was a very well–known expression in the Greek and Roman world. It stood for several things. First, it meant what constitutes a thing at its base. All matter is made up of atoms or particles that cannot be divided further or reduced. The alphabet for language, numbers for arithmetic, notes for the musical scale—all these were called "the elements."

Second, the word signified the elements of particular subjects like anatomy, mechanics, philosophy, science, art, etc., the basic principles out of which we develop our understanding of reality. They are also the given factors on which we base our judgments. We could further speak of the basic principles or elements of religious life, such as the law for the Jews, or more generally the times and acts of worship, festivals, regulations of eating and drinking, doctrines and rules of behavior. What is important about all these elements is that they have to be taken seriously. They are everywhere present, or thought to be present. They are therefore regarded as full of power in the world.

Third, the word was used for the elements of the world—earth, air, fire, water. Some of the planets that were thought to have some impact on life in the world were called "the elements," *stoicheia*. And since days, months, seasons, years were influenced by heavenly bodies, they too came under the power of the elements (4:10). People in the Greek/Roman world felt deeply influenced by all these elements. Thus in the time of Paul, the elements became, in people's minds, superhuman, sometimes demonic powers, controlling life and having human beings in their grip.

The Roman Empire was already showing signs of decline. There were constant conflicts, economic crises, natural disasters. One Roman writer of the time predicted the fall of the empire because "there is no associated enthusiasm of all." There was a loss of self–confidence and of the capacity to control one's self and things. The atmosphere has been described as "a failure of nerve." People were ruled by fear and by Fate and Fortune, considered as capricious gods. So religion flourished—not only the old local pagan cults, but new ones called mystery religions, as well as mixtures of all. Their main function was to find ways of helping people to escape the malign influences of the powers. Astrology became a widespread practice, even by the imperial family itself. Some years after Paul wrote this letter, the Emperor Nero unleashed a massive persecution of Christians in Rome after consulting the astrologers and the elements, *stoicheia*. Peter and Paul both perished in this wave of persecution.

Paul, therefore, chose a very apt phrase to describe an extraordinary paradox. On the one hand, the elements, *stoicheia*, began by being the irreducible elements that make up our world and that we can learn to master by study and reflection. They were the stuff from which human knowledge was acquired and advanced, and by which people could manage themselves and the world. That is, for example, how the mighty Roman Empire came into being. On the other hand, the elements, *stoicheia*, became forces that gained power over people in increasingly irrational ways. The people became slaves to these elements, treating them as gods. And even those who ran the empire became more and more subject to them. This happened in a peculiar way. The emperors, from the time of Augustus (before 14 C.E.), started taking on divine names. Nero would be called "Lord, Savior and Protector of the *oikoumene*," the whole inhabited earth, the empire. At the imperial worship, people had to bow in allegiance to Caesar as god, repeating the divine titles. And then this same Caesar, in his insecurity, consulted the elements, the stars, before embarking on any important enterprise. Making themselves gods, they became subject to gods.

How are we to understand all this today? Certainly, with the benefit of nearly two thousand years, we have acquired an awesome knowledge of the elements of the universe through science. We have learned how to put them to use through technology. We have explored our planet earth and turned it into a global village. We are probing into outer space. We are using up the earth's natural resources, and are producing artificial resources. Our physicists have even broken the atom into smaller elements and gained the secret that went, by human decision, into the production of the atomic bomb. Robert Oppenheimer, the scientific director of the project that produced the first nuclear device, found himself quoting from the Indian religious saga, the *Bhagavadgita,* when he saw the testing of the first bomb: "I am become Death, the shatterer of worlds." This did not prevent President Truman from ordering the bomb dropped on Hiroshima and Nagasaki in August 1945—with the shatteringly deathly results we know. What is worse, after over forty years, the nations, particularly the two competing superpowers, USA and USSR, have continued to produce far more deadly weapons, to such an extent that we can talk of our nuclear policy being MAD (Mutually Assured Destruction).

Yes, we are able to destroy the whole world. So we have a paradox here. The elements in Paul's time were allowed to have superhuman power because people did not yet understand and control them. They did not know how to put them in the total context of their understanding of the world. Two thousand years later we have much more technical mastery over the elements, but we are quite unable to restrain ourselves from proliferating weapons of total destruction because we do not trust one another as human beings and as nations. In the words of that Roman observer, two thousand years ago: "There is no associated enthusiasm of all." We have lost a sense of what we produce because we have lost a sense of the purpose of our existence—to promote life, not death.

This is directly related to our style of life today. Unlike the people in the days of Paul, we have learned, through scientifically based technology, how to produce competitively a vast number of goods. In the process we are using up the earth's resources at an alarmingly rapid pace. We have become the consumer society. "Consumer," according to Webster's dictionary, means "one who spends, uses up, wastes or destroys things." Everything, including people and the environment, have to be sacrificed in order to get the things we must consume from anywhere in the world. So, those things, made of the elements *stoicheia*, become the things that determine our lives. They become gods and idols that we worship instead of the living God.

To have these privileges, we must belong to a powerful state or a powerful group that can command the resources and goods at any cost and make big profits, which we directly or indireclty enjoy. It becomes, therefore, desperately important that our state, or our group be secure and strong in order that we may be protected to consume. So we become a national security, a protectionist state, with our military–industrial complex, our mass media, our ideology of nationalism and power. And all this becomes the most important reality to which we give our allegiance. Our national symbols become slogans of this religious fervor in which the elements have become all–powerful everywhere. Even our religious practices can be occasions when we worship our exclusive and excluding selves as persons and as a people. And unquestionably, religious cults of every kind have been proliferating in these last years. Even particular forms of Christianity have been mobilized to promote and defend our national cgo.

It is in this living context of today that we can understand the truth of Paul's message in these verses (4:8–11). For Paul it was a question of knowing God, or rather being known by God. Paul was here recalling the teaching of the prophets.

Hosea laments the situation of Israel in a manner that is very typical of the prophets, for he evokes the social disorder and the destructive character of the environment:

> Hear the word of the Lord, O people of Israel;
>   for the Lord has an indictment against the
>   inhabitants of the land.
> There is no faithfulness or loyalty,
>   and no knowledge of God in the land;
> Swearing, lying, and murder,
>   and stealing and adultery break out;
>   bloodshed follows bloodshed.
> Therefore the land mourns,
>   and all who live in it languish;
> together with the wild animals
>   and the birds of the air;
>   even the fish of the sea are perishing (Hos. 4:1–3).

Hosea, as God's messenger, proclaims God's word: "I desire steadfast love and not sacrifice, the knowledge of God, rather than burnt offerings" (Hos. 6:6).

An earlier prophet, Amos, attacked what Paul (4:9–10) called the mere religious observance of "days, months, seasons, years":

> Alas for you who desire the day of the Lord!
>   Why do you want the day of the Lord?
> It is darkness, not light . . .
> "I hate, I despise your festivals,
>   and I take no delight in your solemn assemblies.
> Even though you offer me your burnt
>   offerings and grain offerings,
>   I will not accept them;
> and the offerings of well–being of your fatted animals
>   I will not look upon.

Take away from me the noise of your songs;
  I will not listen to the melody of your harps.
But let justice roll down like waters,
  and righteousness like an everflowing stream. (Amos 5:18, 21–24)

The later prophet Jeremiah goes deeper. He calls for an entirely new covenant, with the law becoming a personal experience of knowing God:

The days are surely coming, says the Lord, when I will make a new covenant with the house of Israel and the house of Judah. It will not be like the covenant that I made with their ancestors when I took them by the hand to bring them out of the land of Egypt — a covenant that they broke, though I was their husband, says the Lord. But this is the covenant that I will make with the house of Israel after those days, says the Lord: I will put my law within them, and I will write it on their hearts; and I will be their God, and they shall be my people. No longer shall they teach one another, or say to each other, "Know the Lord," for they shall all know me, from the least of them to the greatest, says the Lord; for I will forgive their iniquity, and remember their sin no more (Jer. 31:31–34).

It is Jeremiah who brings us right back to Paul's controversy with the Galatians. They were being persuaded to give up their direct knowledge of God in Jesus Christ and take on the old covenant and the law with all its requirements. What was needed was a total change of heart towards a totally new experience of knowing the living God. It is to this event that Paul refers in Galatians 4:4–7.

Children of God (4:4–7)

The question is, how can the Galatians and we ourselves be liberated from our captivity to "the elements (*stoicheia*) of the world" and to the religious practices which do not lead to the knowledge of God? Paul goes to the Source of the elements of the world—the Creator God, revealed in Christ the son. When the time had fully come, God sent the son, born within the realm of "the elemental spirits"—born of a woman; born within the sphere of the law that governed the life of Israel, given by God. And the son's mission was to redeem, emancipate, those who were under the law, so that we might receive adoption as sons and daughters of God.

Our understanding of what Paul says can be clarified if we consider what it meant to be "redeemed." The Galatians were well aware of the practice of freeing slaves in the Greek/Roman Empire. The slave or his/her owner would bring the purchase price to the priest at the temple. The money would be paid to the god of the temple. The slave would henceforth belong to the god, but would be a free person in the world. When, therefore, Paul says that Christ redeemed us who were under law or the elemental spirits of the world, he evokes the image of liberation from slavery. A new life begins in which we belong wholly to God. This belonging is the most intimate relationship we can have— being daughters and sons of God. The law and the elemental spirits have no more power over us. They are now discerned to be God's created things. It is God who sets the limits of their place and function, and of our use of them. It is God who also calls us to be responsible for the elements of the world. Paul put this in another way in the greetings to the churches of Galatia:

"Grace and peace to you from God the Father and our Lord Jesus Christ, who gave himself for our sins to deliver us from the present evil age, according to the will of our God and Father" (1:4).

Therefore, we who are redeemed by Christ have a wholly new status in the world. We have quite a different world view. We relate to people and things in a new way. We are no longer enslaved to the law or to the elemental spirits of the world. We are liberated to have right relations with God and with the world God made. We have regained our true calling, as made in God's image, to understand and use the elements of the world for the good of all. We have been given the power to know and to declare with full heart and voice that, at the heart of the universe is not Fate or Fortune, but the Father/Mother. Paul uses a word the Hebrews employed in addressing their earthly father— "*Abba*"("*Imma*" mother). But when they prayed or worshipped publicly, they never addressed God directly as "*Abba*." They would say "*Abi*," "my Father," or "*Abenu*," "our Father." And yet, Jesus did address God in this intimate way: "*Abba*, Father, all things are possible to you; remove this cup from me; yet not what I will, but what you will" (Mk. 14:36). The significance of this saying is that when all the elemental forces of the world, whether religious or political, were ranged against him, Jesus in dark Gethsemane invoked God in the most direct, intimate way. God was the only power that mattered. God would overcome the powers of darkness and turn death into resurrection.

This is what it means to be known by God and to know God (4:8–11). Knowing God is no merely intellectual exercise. It is not just being proficient in grasping "the elements of . . . " whatever constitutes the world of people and things. Knowing God is being in communion with God, and seeing people and things from the perspective and will of God. And to know God we must know Jesus Christ and his liberating work for us on the cross. There the elemental spirits, *stoicheia* of Paul's time and ours, as forces of power over us, are exposed as being "weak and beggarly" (4:9). It is through the power of the risen Christ that we are free to be at the service of God's purpose for the world. And it is through us as children of God that the elements of the world can be transformed to work for the good, the blessing of all.

Pains of Childbirth (4:12–20)

Paul is still wrestling with the question: How is it possible for the Galatians to contemplate relapsing into what they had been before as pagans or falling into a new slavery of trying to observe the whole Mosaic law? "I am afraid for you—that my labor among you in preaching the gospel of freedom in Christ seems to have been in vain, useless" (4:11).

It is on a note of pain and perplexity that Paul opens his heart to the Galatians in affectionate remembrance and in passionate appeal. The extraordinary thing is that when Paul first came to preach the gospel to them, he was in very bad shape physically. Although he looked "weak and beggarly," they did not scorn or despise him. The word for "despise" means "to spit out." Sickness was thought to be caused by evil spirits or demons. People used to spit out on the ground near the afflicted person to ensure not being contaminated. Or, if they felt very superior to the person, they would spit out in a gesture of disdain and disgust. The Galatians did not do that to Paul, far from it. They received him as an angel of God, yes, as Christ Jesus himself. This Jesus was the one who was always beside the sick, the demon possessed, the poor, the outcast, the despised. He became a curse, a cast out for us upon the cross.

"What," asks Paul, "has become of your good feelings towards me? For I testify that, if you could, you would have torn out your eyes and given them to me" (4:15). This was a dramatic way of saying that they would have done anything for him, even if it had deprived them deeply. So then, how could it be that in so relatively short a time, Paul should become their enemy because he told them the truth. "Truth" here certainly means the truth of the gospel. But in Greek the word has the sense of that which is not hidden, covered up, closed. It is that which is in fact brought out into the open, revealed, disclosed about our human existence. Paul was open with them, as he has been in this letter. But what are these other intruding people doing to them? Flattering them? Whatever they are doing, it is to no good end. Instead of opening up the Galatians to the light of life, these intruders want to shut them out from facing the issues of life. They want to gain some short term advantage from the Galatians. As for Paul, he always has had the interests of the Galatians at heart, whether he is present or not. He is not concerned about himself, but about them and the truth of the gospel.

Paul now reveals how profoundly he feels about the Galatians and about his good purpose for them. He calls them, "my little children, with whom I am in the pain of childbirth until Christ is formed in you." He is a mother bearing them all over again in the pains of their birth in the faith, as he did when he first preached to them. And what was his message? "That Christ be formed in you." That they themselves be the womb in which Christ could grow and become life in and for them—not in terms of himself, but that Christ might fill them with his liberating presence. It is to that end that Paul writes and would like to be present with them, and speak to them in the tone of a mother pregnant with love, but alas, he is full of perplexity about them.

Hagar and Sarah (4:21–31)

It would be fitting to end this complicated theological debate with Galatians on that motherly, pastoral note. But Paul's perplexity and restlessness led him to tackle yet another argument used in favor of the Mosaic law. One could wish that Paul could have let it pass and have gone on to the next part of his letter about life in freedom. Instead, he has produced a curious interpretation of an old story, which has perplexed readers, as it might have perplexed the Galatians. Perhaps the explanation for this is that the intruding preachers used the story of Abraham and his two sons to prove their own argument: The Jews and the Jewish Christians, with their adherence to the law, are the descendants of the legitimate son, Isaac. The Gentiles, like the

Galatians, are descendants of the illegitimate son, Ishmael. Hence the need of circumcision as a condition of salvation. How was Paul to deal with this? He decided to use "allegory," a form of interpretation considered to go beyond the obvious meaning of a text to a clearer understanding of God's purpose and promise.

The story itself is told in Genesis 16:1–15; 17:15–26; 21:1–21; 22:15–18. It is a fascinating tale about women and men, about the place of women in the history of salvation, and about the attitudes of women toward each other. But that is not what preoccupied Paul here. Paul's interpretation can be expressed in the following table:[5]

Hagar	Sarah
Ishmael	Isaac
son of the slave woman	son of the free woman
"according to the flesh"	"through the promise"
old covenant	new covenant
Sinai	
present Jerusalem	Jerusalem above
slavery	freedom
"according to the flesh"	"according to the Spirit"
Judaism	Christianity

Paul employs two main arguments. First, Hagar and her circumcised son went to Mount Sinai where the Mosaic law was given. Therefore, following the method of allegory, the Mosaic law is associated with Ishmael, the child born "according to the flesh" (4:24–25). Second, Paul quotes from the prophet of the exile of Israel (Is. 40–55). This book was early regarded as prophesying the new covenant in Christ. The quotation (4:27 from Is. 54:1) speaks of the "childless." In the Genesis story Sarah is described as "childless," *aqarah"* (Gen. 11:30). By God's grace it is she, the childless, despised one who will be more numerous than the one who had the child. Sarah represents the people of the Jerusalem above (4:28). "This means that the future belongs not to law–keeping Jerusalem, but to the company of justified sinners, who, whether Jews or Gentiles in origin, are children of promise."[6]

Paul draws his conclusion. It was traditionally said that the son born according to the flesh, that is, naturally, persecuted the son born by divine intervention, through the Spirit. Paul implies that Jews and Jewish Christians are now harassing the Gentile churches, and so they are excluding themselves from the promise to the people of God. The Galatians must therefore hold their ground as the people of God called by faith to live in freedom (4:29–31).

Women as Rivals

The Sarah–Hagar story is used here as an allegory to prove that Gentiles are included in God's covenant with Abraham and Sarah. It is difficult for us today to follow easily such allegoric interpretation. However, the story of Sarah and Hagar is interesting and important from a woman's perspective. It contains a classical conflict between women as rivals with each other over childbearing. In a challenging interpretation, Elsa Tamez has seen the two women representing First World (Sarah) and Third World (Hagar).[7] Hagar, the slave girl, works for her mistress Sarah who must have some status and property. Therefore she can "use" Hagar according to her will. This was the norm in patriarchal, slaveholding societies. Women today have to take notice that there are deep differences between women by class and race and we cannot quickly pretend that this is not so. Tamez sees Hagar as the woman "who complicated the history of salvation." The plain, straight–forward line from Abraham and Sarah to the people of Israel is interrupted and complicated by the presence of Hagar and her son Ishmael. Tamez sees this as a story in which God is putting a poor slave girl on the map of human history, into the history of salvation. This might encourage us to think about our understanding of women. Paul made use of the story to include Gentiles in the history of salvation and to that end he favored Sarah. He saw her as barren and oppressed by the exile situation, but receiving a sign of grace. Maybe today we have to learn to look again to discover whom we should include in the history of salvation. We need to discover what the marginal people in the biblical stories do for us by challenging us in our "comfortable" faith.—*B.W.P.*

5. Freedom in the Spirit

Galatians

5 For freedom Christ has set us free. Stand firm, therefore, and do not submit again to a yoke of slavery.

2 Listen! I, Paul, am telling you that if you let yourselves be circumcised, Christ will be of no benefit to you. ³Once again I testify to every man who lets himself be circumcised that he is obliged to obey the entire law. ⁴You who want to be justified by the law have cut yourselves off from Christ; you have fallen away from grace. ⁵For through the Spirit, by faith, we eagerly wait for the hope of righteousness. ⁶For in Christ Jesus neither circumcision nor uncircumcision counts for anything; the only thing that counts is faith working through love.

7 You were running well; who prevented you from obeying the truth? ⁸Such persuasion does not come from the one who calls you. ⁹A little yeast leavens the whole batch of dough. ¹⁰I am confident about you in the Lord that you will not think otherwise. But whoever it is that is confusing you will pay the penalty. ¹¹But my frineds, why am I still being persecuted if I am still preaching circumcision? In that case the offense of the cross has been removed. ¹²I wish those who unsettle you would castrate themselves!

13 For you were called to freedom, brothers and sisters; only do not use your freedom as an opportunity for self–indulgence, but through love become

slaves to one another. [14]For the whole law is summed up in a single commandment, "You shall love your neighbor as yourself." [15]If, however, you bite and devour one another, take care that you are not consumed by one another.

16 Live by the Spirit, I say, and do not gratify the desires of the flesh. [17]For what the flesh desires is opposed to the Spirit, and what the Spirit desires is opposed to the flesh; for these are opposed to each other, to prevent you from doing what you want. [18]But if you are led by the Spirit, you are not subject to the law. [19]Now the works of the flesh are obvious: fornication, impurity, licentiousness, [20]idolatry, sorcery, enmities, strife, jealousy, anger, quarrels, dissensions, factions, [21]envy, drunkenness, carousing, and things like these. I am warning you, as I warned you before: those who do such things will not inherit the kingdom of God.

22 By contrast, the fruit of the Spirit is love, joy, peace, patience, kindness, generosity, faithfulness, [23]gentleness, and self–control. There is no law against such things. [24]And those who belong to Christ Jesus have crucified the flesh with its passions and desires.

25 If we live by the Spirit, let us also be guided by the Spirit. [26]Let us not become conceited, competing against one another, envying one another.

Freed from the Yoke of Slavery (5:1–12)

"For freedom Christ has set us free. Stand firm, therefore, and do not submit again to a yoke of slavery" (5:1). This and the following verses sum up what Paul has been writing to the Galatians in the previous chapters. From the very

72

beginning of the letter (2:4–5), Paul has been struggling with the Galatians to guard the freedom they have received in the gospel of Jesus Christ. The whole purpose of the grace of God revealed in Christ has been to liberate us from "the present evil world" (1:4); "from the curse (doom) of the law" (3:13); and from "the elemental spirits of the world" (4:3). By our faith–commitment to Christ we are made not only free for God and in ourselves, but we become free for one another. The barriers of race, class and sex are broken down (3:28). Christ has enabled us through the Spirit to draw near to God as our Father/Mother and to each other as sisters and brothers. The world is no longer alien and hostile. It has become a place where all can be at home in the family of God (4:1–7). *CHRISTIANS + NONCHRIST ?*

Paul does not waste time in stating the fact of our freedom. What matters is that we keep on standing firm and do not submit again to a yoke of slavery. Freedom is never static. We either grow in freedom or we fall back into the slavery of legalism or licentious living or both. The founders of the American republic understood this well when they declared, fought for and gained their liberty as a nation. One of them, Thomas Jefferson, said: "The price of liberty is eternal vigilance." What, for Christians, is the nature of this freedom and "eternal vigilance"?

Paul starts by warning the Galatians once again that there is nothing to be gained by compromising their freedom with the seduction of being circumcised and living by the law. They would be separating themselves from Christ, the source of their freedom, and from grace, the self–giving love of God. Rather they are encouraged to live out their hopes as the Spirit empowers them, so that righteousness—right relations with God, with people and with creation—will become more of a reality. Neither circumcision nor uncircumcision matters. What makes all the difference is faith functioning daily and concretely in love.

Paul is irritated that the good beginning of the Galatians in Christian freedom is being eroded by those teachers who are standing in the way of their freedom. He quotes an old

proverb: "A little yeast leavens the whole batch of dough."
This was a reference to the Jewish law that prohibited the
use of leaven during the seven days of the feast of the
Passover—the most sacred festival of remembrance of the
Israelites' liberation from slavery in Egypt (Ex. 12:14–20;
Deut. 16:3–8). Leaven became a symbol of what can invade
and become corrupting and destructive. Paul applies this
meaning of the symbol to circumcision and the law.

Paul is horrified that the Galatians are moving away from
the message of "the offense of the cross" (5:11b). It was
because of this message that he who had persecuted the
Christians was himself persecuted (see 2 Cor. 11:22–23). It
was this message that they had received and which had
given them a new life of freedom. Paul wishes that those
who are doing so much harm would "castrate themselves"
(5:12). These may be very harsh words, but they make their
point. In Paul's time, a castrated person could not function
as a practicing Jew, nor could a castrated person become
circumcised and therefore a Jew. Paul is using a dramatic
phrase to say that those who are unsettling the Galatians
should leave them alone once and for all. The Galatians
have far more important business to attend to.

Freed for Mutual Love (5:13–15)

"For you were called to freedom, brothers and sisters; only
do not use your freedom as an opportunity for self-indul-
gence [the flesh], but through love become slaves to one
another." Freedom is not only a fact, a condition of our
existence, but a calling, a task. To be liberated is to participate in the process of liberation. And this liberated life
expresses itself in liberating love in the community of faith
and to all around us and beyond.

Paul is at least showing some sensitivity to the dilemma
the Galatians faced. He himself admits that they had been
exceptionally kind and receptive to him and his message
(4:12–15). What, then went wrong? Up to now Paul puts all

the weight of his debate with the Galatians on the intruders from outside who were trying to impose circumcision and the law. But the Galatians were only human. They had come out of a pagan background and still lived in that pagan environment. Paul had preached to them and had probably given them some general guidelines about how they should conduct themselves as Christians. He had left them the Greek version of the Hebrew Testament (what we commonly refer to as the Old Testament), which the literate could read. But they had no New Testament as we have, including this letter to them. At least, in the Hebrew Testament there were the commandments and other directives that regulated the moral, physical and worshipping life.

The moral teaching of the Greeks was largely confined to the philosophical schools and to the mystery religions, which demanded initiation rites. The relatively new converts probably felt that it was better to observe the Jewish moral code than fall back into the past pagan cult and culture, though they were hardly conscious of the danger of slipping into a self–righteous legalism, especially those who might be literate and were leaders (see Gal. 5:26–6:5).

It was perhaps at this point that the opposing preachers came in and sought to convince the Galatians that if they were going to observe the moral code in the Mosaic law they might as well be circumcised and observe the whole law, as a condition of being Christian. Was Paul himself not a practicing Jew as well as a Christian? So the Galatians felt they were caught between following the way of the law and going their own way, "doing their own thing" as each thought fit. Being together in a new community of faith was no easy matter with people of different classes, sexes, races and opinions. The tensions must have been quite severe. The community faced the risk of falling apart; the conflict of selfish wills could only end in mutual destruction. Paul recognized this and warned: "If you bite and devour one another, take care that you are not consumed by one another" (5:15).

This is the context in which Paul tells the Galatians that

their calling to be free persons is a call to be "slaves" one of another in love. That is in conformity with the commandment: "You shall love your neighbor as yourself" (Lev. 19:18b). That, says Paul paradoxically, is the command that fulfills the whole law—paradoxically, because we cannot become free persons by trying to fulfill the law. Paul was emphatic about this. How can we understand it?

When Paul was a fervent Jewish scholar he had probably heard that Rabbi Hillel had summed up the law in terms of Leviticus 19:18b, and had exhorted a possible proselyte: "What is hateful to you, do not to your neighbor; that is the whole law; everything else is commentary; go and learn it."[8] Of course, Paul would also have heard the more positive version of this golden rule from the teaching of Jesus: "In everything do to others as you would have them do to you: for this is the law and the prophets" (Mt. 7:12). Paul would also have known that Jesus brought together the two Jewish commandments to love God and love the neighbor (Deut. 6:4–5; Lev. 19:18b), and had said: "There is no other commandment greater than these" (Mk. 12:31). Paul, therefore, felt free, in the spirit of Jesus, to offer the Galatians, by way of guidance, what was the essence of the Mosaic law, which Jesus himself embodied and deepened. He could speak thus because the Galatians would respond according to their faith in Christ and their willingness to be guided by the Spirit.

It is also true that the rabbis had a beautiful comment on Leviticus 19:18b: "You shall love your neighbor as yourself: I am the Lord." They would say, on the last words, "I am the Lord": "Remember, when poor persons are at your gate, the Lord (YHWH) is beside them." It was, however, Jesus who, in telling the parable of the Good Samaritan, pointed out that a neighbor was not just a fellow Jew, or one who was not unclean, but any human being in need (Lk. 10:25–37). Paul said the same to the Galatians (6:10), and later to the Romans (Rom. 13:8–10). Those who have been freed by Christ at the cost of the cross can have the same freedom to turn what was given as law, with all its limitations, into daily attitude and act, in the power of the Spirit.

The other paradox in this call to act in freedom is, in Paul's terminology, that through love we are to become slaves of one another. Can love be a call to slavery? Paul has thundered against the slavery of the law. Yet, when he started his letter to the Galatians, he said: "If I were still pleasing people, I would not be a servant [slave] of Christ" (1:10). On the face of it, a slave was one who was expected to please the owner and those around. Paul rejected this attitude; so what does he mean by "slave of Christ"? Some time later, while he was in prison in Rome, Paul wrote an affectionate letter to the Philippians. He exhorted them: "Do nothing from selfish ambition or conceit, but in humility regard others as better than yourselves. Let each of you look not to your own interests, but to the interests of others" (Phil. 2:3–4). And then he went on to say: "Let the same mind be in you that was in Christ Jesus,

who, though he was in the form of God,
    did not regard equality with God
    as something to be exploited, [or harped upon]
but emptied himself,
    taking the form of a slave,
    being born in human likeness.
And being found in human form,
    he humbled himself
    and became obedient to the point of death—
    even death on a cross" (Phil. 2:5–8).

Just as Jesus became a curse for us to liberate us from our curse (doom) (Gal. 3:13), so he became human in the most humiliating state, a slave. He did that in order that he might free us from our slavery to our selfishness in order that we might become self–giving, disregarding any status or rank we might have. Here, then, is real freedom at work—giving ourselves in love, whatever may be the cost. To be truly free is to be at the disposal of others. That is what the gospel of freedom is about.

No one understood all this more clearly and more eloquently than the reformer, Martin Luther. One of his earliest sayings in 1516 was: "The will of a person without grace is not free, but slavish." After he had posted his ninety–five theses on the door of the church in Wittenberg on 11 November 1517 (which sparked off the Reformation), he signed himself in twenty–seven known letters, "Martinus Eleutherius"—"Martin the Free Man." In 1520 he published a tract on "The Freedom of the Christian." At the beginning he writes:

A Christian is the most free lord of all, and subject to none.
A Christian is the most willing servant of all, and subject to everyone.[9]

That was the spirit in which the Reformation broke out in the early sixteenth century. We are the inheritors of this freedom of the Christian to be both subject to no one save Christ, and the willing servant of all in the name of Christ. Over four hundred years after, following World War II, the German philosopher, Karl Jaspers, wrote an essay in which he was reflecting on the Nazi tyranny in his country. He concluded his reflections with these words: "No one is free who does not work for the freedom of others."

Where Do We Stand?

I cannot read and comment on Paul's great utterances on freedom, liberation in Christ, without emotion. On the eve of emancipation in the English–speaking Caribbean on 1 August 1834, slaves gathered in the Baptist, Moravian and Methodist chapels to receive their freedom not from some government official, but from Christ. The text read was precisely Galatians 5:1, 13–14. After four years of "apprenticeship," my fore-

78

parents were free in the sense that they were no longer the property of anyone.

In 1988, we celebrated the one hundred and fiftieth anniversary of this liberation. We asked ourselves in what way were we really free. The end of slavery was not the end of economic and social oppression. The whole plantation system remained in place, backed by laws passed by the white legislatures. In 1937–38, there were uprisings all over the Caribbean. The British Government responded by sending a Royal Commission to hear the complaints of the people. The results were welfare measures without racial, political or social changes. The struggle went on till the 1960s and 1970s when most of the Caribbean territories got their political independence. But there was little sustained change because economic power was still in the hands of great oligarchies and of the powerful industrialized nations.

We may have some measure of liberty according to the law, but we are not liberated from economic and social oppression. Moreover, we find ourselves, as we have been from the sixteenth century, part of the "web of oppression" that grips our brothers and sisters in Africa, Asia and Latin America. And we are in solidarity with the deprived and the poor in the rich countries, like the USA. Because we are so divided economically, racially and socially, we are constantly biting and devouring one another. Paul is prophetic in warning us that if we continue on this course around the world, we will be consumed by one another (5:15).

There has been much questioning and criticism of the attempt at articulating, in the footsteps of Paul, a theology of liberation by Black Americans, Latin Americans, West Indians, Africans, Asians and Women. This theology starts with the gospel of liberation and the call to all to be servants one of another through love. This theology notes that Jesus our liberator showed a clear solidarity with the poor, the op-

pressed, the marginalized, in the spirit of the prophets. He gave them all a sense of identity and dignity as
persons. This theology follows the tradition of the
prophets in analyzing and judging the social, economic and political structures of our societies in the light of
God's righteousness, God's justice. This theology calls
us all to bear one another's burdens and work for true
human dignity and community in Spirit—a world
community of caring and sharing.

We must therefore ask ourselves where we stand as
Christians and as Christian communities in the struggle of people, at home and abroad, for a more just and
equitable society. This is an essential part of our faith
in Christ, our liberator.—*P.P.*

Living by the Spirit or the Flesh? (5:16–23)

Our call to be free in ourselves and for others is not
something we can do by our own human powers alone. No
one knew this better than Paul himself. He quickly says to
the Galatians: "Live by the Spirit, I say, and do not gratify
the desires of the flesh." Spirit and flesh are opposed to
each other in an unending conflict. Both of these words and
realities have been popping up in our reading of this letter.

"Flesh" in this letter is used in two distinct senses. One is
our existence as bodily, mortal beings (1:16; 2:20; 4:23).
The other connotes egoism, self-assertion, self-indul-
gence, the whole self which is at war with God, with ourselves and with the world (3:3; 5:13, 16–19; 6:8, 12). It is
another way of speaking about sin. Martin Luther described it as being *incurvatus in se*, wrapped up into one's
self. The best way to understand "flesh" is to understand
that to which it is opposed—the Spirit. Here we come to the
center of our faith: the Spirit of God present with power
to create, renew, bestow gifts. It is the Spirit who unwraps

80

and unravels us from our closed, dark existence and enables us to stand erect with the risen Christ. Paul writes to the Corinthians: "The Lord is the Spirit, and where the Spirit of the Lord is, there is freedom" (2 Cor. 3:17).

The Galatians had experienced this power when Paul first preached Christ to them (3:3, 5). It is the Spirit who confirms in believers the promise of the blessing through Abraham (3:14). It is the Spirit who enables us to pray and call God, *Abba* (4:6). It is the Spirit who sustains us in hope and right relations with God and others (5:5).

No wonder that Martin Luther could describe the life of faith as *coram Deo*, before God. It is this unwrapped presence before God and before our neighbors in love that is the great gift of the Spirit.

So we are caught in the outer and inner battles between the drives of our flesh and the guiding of the Spirit. Our freedom in Christ is never assured. It is constantly threatened. Therefore, we had better, like the Galatians, face up to the stark alternatives, and what is involved in them.

Paul gives a list of the work, the concrete acts, that life under the desires of the flesh produces. This list is a very old one. The Galatians knew it well in their Gentile world. So do we. When we read the list in the context of our freedom in Christ, it is frighteningly real. It is as if we are looking at ourselves in a mirror.

The following observations can be made about the list (5:19–21). (1) What predominate are vices that belong to our attitudes and personal and community relationships—enmities, strife, jealousy, anger, quarrels, dissensions, factions, envy. It is these vices of heart and mind that propel us to licentious and violent acts. (2) The sensual vices begin and end the list—fornication, impurity, licentiousness, drunkenness, carousing, etc. (3) Two are in the religious realm—one is idolatry, the elevation of things, systems, and even persons to be gods we worship; the other is sorcery, taking things or beings and investing them with evil power so as to manipulate others. What comes through is the divisive and destructive nature of these attitudes and acts of self–will and self–indulgence. That is why they are called "works," not "work." They are the kinds of attitudes and actions that lead to persons and communities being consumed, annihilated by one another (5:15). They describe the character of the "the present evil age" (1:4).

The other list is made up of the "fruit," not "fruits," of the Spirit. Already the image is an organic one, suggesting that all things are related to each other. It is a shorter, well–ordered, and compact list, which can be divided into three parts: (1) Love, joy, peace—those fundamental qualities that undergird and direct our existence in freedom. (2) Patience, kindness, goodness/generosity—practical attitudes and acts that build up community. (3) Faithfulness/reliability, gentleness, self–control—the ways in which we endure and weather the storms of passion and self–will.

There are three comments that can be made of this list:

(1) The clearest impression is that all these manifestations of the fruit of the Spirit are community–creating and sustaining.

(2) In the Greek codes of moral behavior, two of these graces are conspicuously absent—love and goodness. Love, *agape*, was a seldom used Greek word that was adopted by Jews and Christians to express the love of God that is willed, constant and unwavering. By contrast, Plato and other philosophers and moralists gave the highest place to self–control. For them self–control is a quality one has in one's self and for one's self. For Paul, self–control comes from our being upheld and directed by the Spirit and it is self–control for the sake of self–giving. The philosphers spoke of the good as a state to aim at. The Greek Old Testament and subsequently the New Testament use the word "goodness," not as a state to be attained, but as a disposition to express in concrete ways the goodness of God, which is new every moment of our lives.

(3) Except for the exuberant joy (*chara* in Greek, related to *charis*, grace), these "fruit of the Spirit" have a quiet, unfussy and down–to–earth quality about them. They go to the heart of the business of living from moment to moment

in open–minded freedom. It is new life in Christ daily conducted in the presence of God. It is not an ideal, inner, exceptional or heroic life. It is life in the flesh, radically transformed and given a new direction.

Paul ends this catalog of "the fruit of the Spirit" with the statement: "There is no law against such things." No code of law can bring about such interrelated, organic qualities. Law gives the general direction to what we may do and not do. It threatens, condemns, demands. It is like our legal systems. They provide a framework within which a society may seek to be sanely constituted; but they cannot make our society just or loving. Indeed, human passions and desires find all sorts of ways of being unjust within the law by going around the law. The most the law can do, in effect, is to limit in some fashion the results of "the works of the flesh" by agreed–upon punishing measures. "It is more important to be enabled to act with ethical responsibility than to introduce a code of law which remains a mere demand."[10]

It is interesting to note the contrast between what is said at the end of the list of "the fruit of the Spirit" and what Paul says at the end of the list of "the works of the flesh." He asserts, in a solemn warning: "Those who do such things will not inherit the kingdom of God" (5:21b). In his letter to the Corinthians, Paul writes: "Do you not know that wrongdoers [the unrighteous/unjust] will not inherit the kingdom of God?" And he goes on to give a list of such persons (1 Cor. 6:9–10). Certainly, the Mosaic law, especially as interpreted by the prophets, would condemn "the works of the law." But it is instructive to reflect on how Jesus viewed the matter:

Not every one who says to me, "Lord, Lord," will enter the kingdom of heaven, but only the one who does the will of my Father in heaven. On that day many will say to me, "Lord, Lord, did we not prophesy in your name, and cast out demons in your name and do many deeds of power in your name?" Then I will declare to them, "I never knew you; go away from me, you evildoers" (Mt. 7:21–23).

Jesus is reminding his hearers that, at the final reckoning, what counts is not strict observance of the law (Mt. 5:21–48), or even individual acts that may be in line with Jesus' teaching. What finally counts is our inner disposition, the unself-conscious qualities that make up "the fruit of the Spirit." Here law is transformed into love through the Spirit.

Where Do We Belong? (5:24)

"Those who belong to Christ Jesus have crucified the flesh with its passions and desires." These words explain the content of "the fruit of the Spirit." If indeed "the fruit of the Spirit" is so abundant, if the law is transcended by it, it is because it is embodied in persons who belong to Jesus Christ. Crucifying the flesh is putting all our self-regard and self-will, with the passions and desires that spring from them, at the foot of the cross. It is an act of self-surrender to Christ, leaving behind us our human securities. It is a determination to accept the challenge of Christ to deny ourselves, take up our cross and follow him daily. Here is the true basis for our ethical existence. This is so fundamental to Paul that he makes the same affirmation of self-surrender at the beginning and at the end of this letter (2:19b–20 and 6:14). It has been truly said that for Paul "the cross is the final explanation of everything Christian."

The price of liberty is only, in the *second* place, eternal vigilance of ourselves before our daily reality. In the *first* place, it is eternal vigil in communion with our crucified and risen liberator, Jesus Christ.

6 Bear One Another's Burdens

6 My friends, if anyone is detected in a transgression, you who have received the Spirit should restore such a one in a spirit of gentleness. Take care that you yourselves are not tempted. ²Bear one another's burdens, and in this way you will fulfill the law of Christ. ³For if those who are nothing think they are something, they deceive themselves. ⁴All must test their own work; then that work, rather than their neighbor's work, will become a cause for pride. ⁵For all must carry their own loads.

6 Those who are taught the word must share in all good things with their teacher.

7 Do not be deceived; God is not mocked, for you reap whatever you sow. ⁸If you sow to your own flesh, you will reap corruption from the flesh; but if you sow to the Spirit, you will reap eternal life from the Spirit. ⁹So let us not grow weary in doing what is right, for we will reap at harvest–time, if we do not give up. ¹⁰So then, whenever we have an opportunity, let us work for the good of all, and especially for those of the family of faith.

11 See what large letters I make when I am writing in my own hand! ¹²It is those who want to make a good showing in the flesh that try to compel you to be circumcised—only that they may not be persecuted for the cross of Christ. ¹³Even the circumcised do not themselves obey the law, but they want you to be circumcised so that they may boast

about your flesh. [14]May I never boast of anything except the cross of our Lord Jesus Christ, by which the world has been crucified to me, and I to the world. [15]For neither circumcision nor uncircumcision is anything; but a new creation is everything! [16]As for those who will follow this rule—peace be upon them, and mercy, and upon the Israel of God.

17 From now on, let no one make trouble for me; for I carry the marks of Jesus branded on my body.

18 May the grace of our Lord Jesus Christ be with your spirit, brothers and sisters. Amen.

Paul has arrived at the point where he wants to speak heart to heart with the Galatian churches about their life together as believers and in the communities in which they live. He has had to establish his credentials and his authority as apostle and as their missionary and brother in the faith. He has had to debate with them, and with those preachers and teachers who had come to unsettle them, about the dangers of lapsing into slavery to a legal system. He has just reminded them that their true life in Christ is one of freedom—freedom to live as joyful children in the presence of God the Father/Mother; freedom to be themselves as those who have come of age; freedom to be at the service of one another; freedom to live creatively by the guidance of the Spirit; freedom to place their lives wholly at the disposal of Christ.

Living a New Life (5:25–6:5)

Now, Paul places himself beside the Galatians as he says: "If we live by the Spirit, let us also be guided by the Spirit." The verb for "guide" has the same root as the noun for "the elemental spirits" (*stoicheia*). (See 4:3–11.) The Galatians would know that the Greeks used it to mean "following someone's principles of thinking and acting," "walking in step with someone." It is the Spirit of God in Christ who will accompany us along the way of faith working through love. It is therefore entirely out of place for us to be "conceited," literally, "emptily–opinionated"—showing off ourselves over against others, while in fact we have little or nothing to show. Nor should we "compete against one another" in a provocative way. Nor should we be envious of one another. Such things are "works of the flesh." They poison relations and threaten the very fabric of the community (5:15). These attitudes can manifest themselves in all relationships—marriage, the family, the local congregation, at work and in the community.

What, then, is to be done? Paul uses a very ordinary, normal occurrence. What do we do when someone has been found doing wrong? Do we immediately charge that person, and call for summary judgment and punishment? Paul says to us: Be careful! Watch your step! This person is a fallible human being like you. It could be you next time. Rather, as a person who is guided by the Spirit, you must show to this wrongdoer that precious fruit of the Spirit—gentleness (5:23). Seek to restore this person to the community, set him/her on the right course. "Gentleness" means "controlled strength," a quality that one employs not to deny, but to affirm the other. It helps to put the other in a frame of mind to be assisted to resume the journey of life with the Spirit. Jesus used that very word, gentleness, when he said: "Blessed are the meek [gentle], for they will inherit the earth" (Mt. 5:5). Again Jesus says: "Come to me, all you who are weary and are carrying heavy burdens and I will give you rest. Take my yoke upon you, and learn from me, for I am gentle [meek] and humble in heart, and you will find rest for your souls. For my yoke is easy [kind] and my burden is light" (Mt. 11:28–30).

What is important to note is that Paul is more concerned with how the community deals with the wrong–doer than what it does about the wrong deed. A great church leader of the fourth century C.E., John Chrysostom, remarked: "Paul does not say, 'punish,' or 'condemn,' but 'set right.'" We must be constantly aware that our Christian life is ambiguous and threatened, and is always in process of becoming. "One test of true spirituality is a readiness to set those who stumble by the wayside on the right road again in a sympathetic and uncensorious spirit."[11]

Hence Paul can say to us all: "Keep on bearing one another's burdens, and in this way you will fulfill the law of Christ." This means burdens of every kind—physical, economic, emotional, moral, etc. What is of interest about the word "burdens" is that it signifies things that are too heavy for one person to carry alone. Paul implies that we all, in different forms, carry burdens beyond our strength. We need one another. That is the true life in the Spirit, the freedom to serve one another in love. We must not miss the significance of this advice in the context of Paul's argument with his opponents. The same word "burden" occurs in a saying of Jesus in which he challenges the scribes and Pharisees who are guardians of the law: "They tie up heavy burdens, hard to bear, and lay them on [the] shoulders of others; but they themselves are unwilling to lift a finger to move them" (Mt. 23:4). That would explain why Paul adds to his advice, "in this way you will fulfill the law of Christ." It also explains his declaration: "The whole law is summed up in a single commandment: 'You shall love your neighbor as yourself'" (5:14).

There is in fact only one law of Christ, and this law is not law but the offer of a way of life, freely accepted by those who follow Christ and are guided by the Spirit. Everything about ourselves, about our life together as Christian communities with the wider community that lays its claims on us, yes, everything can be summed up in one sentence: "Keep on bearing one another's burdens."

Solidarity—At the Heart of Faith

In 1976 South Africa was shaken by the protest of the Black students, which led on June 16 to the killing by riot police of eleven–year–old Hector Petersen and many other students. This was the beginning of another wave of police oppression. The white government lashed out at the black community as it struggled against apartheid.

A year later, the German Christian Women's Movement recommended to its members a boycott of South African fruits and products. I was part of this initiative. We wanted to withdraw our support from the profitable trade between West Germany and South Africa. We thought that women have at least the "power of the shopping bag," if no other. So we started to make our voices heard—and we were inspired by Paul's word, "Bear one another's burdens, and in this way you will fulfill the law of Christ." In the years since then, many people, church organizations and countries have taken up the challenge to boycott apartheid. The German women were only a small part in a long chain. But in my church they were a crucial force.

love your neighbor?

Some questions kept coming up like: "Should Christians be involved in something that looks like a political action? Why do we choose South Africa? Do such protests have any effect?"

If we look at our world at large, the problems are quite overwhelming and one does not know where to start and where to end. Many people have abandoned public responsibility altogether and accommodated themselves in private and pious corners. But what is the result? Life might be more quiet and comfortable, but it is also exempted from the vital elements of our faith. It becomes a "soft cushion" or a "dry bone." But faith is meant to be "salt" and "light" for the world;

it is meant to be a vital force in our personal life and community life. That is why we cannot but respond to the cries of the suffering around us and bear one another's burdens.

The German women, as many people in this country, experienced that as soon as they got involved in real issues, the puzzling feelings of helplessness and dullness disappeared. We *could* do indeed a lot of things. It began with exposing even more women to the facts of apartheid. The women began to learn what apartheid means and how it functions—and in the process they discovered how deeply our own country is implicated in the apartheid system—by trade, by exploiting black labor, by political support to the regime.

Learning was the first step in bearing one another's burdens. Even in our free societies the news media reports are very selective and often deprive us of a true understanding of the issues. This prevents us from developing a global sensitivity to one another. In Germany, after a period of learning, many initiatives sprang up, in the churches and in society at large. Others began to join in and today apartheid is under considerable pressure from outside.

Does it really make a difference whether we involve ourselves in the global issues, in solidarity work? The United Methodist Church invites its members every year to learn and study global issues and hear the voices of people from all over the world. The church then proposes concrete steps that might be taken in solidarity with people who are oppressed. Some insights from this involvement might be useful to discuss:

● We should listen to the voices of the people in the situation, be it in South Africa or elsewhere, and understand what they say and what they want. We must not hurry to impose our own solutions.

● We cannot feel pity for a black child in a township

without asking: How can apartheid be ended? What role can we play in it?

• The Bible tells us the story of the mustard seed and many other stories of small beginnings. We learn from such stories that smallness, small numbers, is not a hindrance in seeking God's kingdom. It is the purposeful, faithful participation that makes a difference.

• Whether we involve ourselves in South Africa, or in a neighborhood program for battered women, for minorities or for Central America does not really matter, as long as we see that things are connected and support the efforts of others.

• It really makes a difference at the end of the day to pray to God: "See our small steps of faithfulness" rather than cry out "Why does God allow this to happen"? God might return the question and ask us: "Why do *you* allow this to happen"? To bear one another's burdens is to fulfill the law of Christ. Solidarity is not accidental but at the heart of our faith and faithfulness. United Methodist women in this country have given outstanding support and leadership in global solidarity. Let us strengthen and support these efforts. It really does make a difference for those in despair in many parts of the world to know that in one of the most powerful countries of the world the voices and actions of the family of faith, in solidarity with one another, must be reckoned with.—*B.W.P.*

Help Us to Help Each Other

I learned a great deal about "bearing one another's burdens" while I was a pastor in Cap Haitien in the north of Haiti from 1950 to 1954. I was the first black pastor of the Methodist Church to go to work among the Haitians. The people I ministered to were among the poorest of the poor in Haiti and in the Americas.

Ninety percent of them could not read or write. Many of the members of the village churches had been actively involved in Voodoo practices before receiving the gospel of liberation in Christ. During my second visit to one of the villages, I had to go through the membership role with the church leaders. When we came to the name of a woman who lived closeby, I was told that it should be removed from the roll. I asked why. There was silence. I persisted. Gradually I learned that she had been to see the Voodoo doctor and had ceased to come to the church. So once more I asked why.

Eventually it came out that three of this woman's children had died within a few months. She had lacked money to go to the medical doctor, and had decided in desperation to go to the Voodoo doctor. Then I asked: "Where were you when this woman was going through this great distress? Were you beside her to help and confort her?" There was uncomfortable silence. After a while we prayed about the sad situation, and for the woman and her family. The church community realized they had not behaved as sisters and brothers in Christ. They had failed to show love to a sister in need. We decided to visit and assist this sister. It took time for her to regain confidence in herself and in the Christian community. But in time, she did. She became an active member of the church and of the village community.

Soon we got to work as a village in helping the people fix their small houses and also in making the small wooden chapel a place of meeting and recreation. It became a delight to go to this village. Every time I preached to the congregation in this and in other villages, I would tell them stories from my ecumenical experiences and travels, as well as from my readings about the people and the churches of the world. We always prayed for the worldwide community of Christians. This was the high point in a worship service or church meeting. Then on one occasion I had heard over the British broadcasting network (BBC) that there were terrible floods in India. Many had died, and many more were homeless. I told the congregation about India and the condition of the people. I told them about the work of the church and of all the interchurch aid and various relief services available through the World Council of Churches. The following week I received a delegation from all the congregations. They said they had prayed about the people in India and had considered what they should do. They handed me the equivalent of U.S. eleven dollars. The tears ran down my cheeks as I saw in their eyes this token of bearing one another's burdens.

I was reminded of Charles Wesley's hymn:

Help us to help each other, Lord
Each other's cross to bear;
Let each the friendly aid afford,
and feel the other's care.

—*P.P.*

Verses 3 and 4 of chapter 6 are really an expansion of what Paul had already written in chapter 5, verse 26. The greatest danger for us as persons, as communities, and as nations, is to have and express superior attitudes towards others; to set ourselves up as the standard by which people and things are judged; to be self–righteous. What is worse is that we do not trouble to watch ourselves and judge ourselves even by the standards we set and use against others. Bearing one another's burdens can degenerate into minding other people's business. What Paul is telling us is that we can only bear one another's burdens if we all carry our own load.

The word for "load" means one's tools, outfit, fishing

gear, baggage. Each of us has a certain ability with the appropriate equipment. We have to exercise this ability with a sense of responsibility and integrity. This primary meaning can be expanded to include other responsibilities, which everybody has in the community. Perhaps the best analogy for both "Bear one another's burdens" and "all must carry their own loads" is Paul's image of the body and its members in 1 Corinthians 12:12–27. Each member—hand, eye, ear, etc.—has its own identity and function. But no part is independent of the rest of the body. There should be "no dissension within the body," but the members should have "the same care for one another. If one member suffers, all suffer together with it; if one member is honored, all rejoice together" (1 Cor. 12:25–26). In that same letter Paul speaks of the variety of gifts of the Spirit available to the Christian community. While each has its special function, "to each is given the manifestation of the Spirit for the common good" (1 Cor. 12:7–11).

In these few counsels Paul is very wisely and skillfully helping us to understand what freedom is all about. We are liberated by Christ from all that prevents us from being ourselves as persons made in God's image, and as unique individuals having beauty, dignity and indestructible value. The guidance of the Spirit enables us to discern what the choices in life are, in the course of our concrete, daily movements and encounters. But it is we who have to decide, we who have to respond to our situation in a responsible way. It is this responding and responsibility that is called "faith" in the Bible. It is the free, voluntary decision to be faithful, reliable, committed. It is our capacity to say *Amen* to the God before whom we live: "I believe you; I put myself, my life at your disposal." But our decision is always taken in confronting two paths—one, "the works of the flesh," and the other, "the fruit of the Spirit." The one is the path of the destruction of ourselves and of the community. The other is the path of growing as persons and as part of a community with the qualities ranging from love to self-control, all as an integrated whole (5:22–23). And this we do as a community of faith—of mutual respect, correction, caring and sharing.

There is another perspective in these two directives. At the end of the list of "the works of the flesh," Paul warns: "Those who do such things will not inherit the kingdom of God" (5:21). Our freedom is not abstract, static, neutral or directionless. It is part of our pilgrimage towards the final reckoning. Paul uses, only here in this letter, an old expression, "the kingdom of God"—the sovereign rule of God, which is righteousness. This Christ taught us to seek (Mt. 6:33). In Matthew's gospel, the last collection of Jesus' teachings before the record of his passion, death and resurrection, are the three parables of the kingdom of heaven (Mt. 25). The first two parables of the wise and foolish virgins, and of the wise and foolish servants, show whether and how people carry their own load—doing what they are supposed to do, what they are fitted to do, what is in their power to do, or not. In the last parable, the scene of the final judgment, we are asked whether or not we have borne the burdens of the hungry, the thirsty, the stranger, the naked, the sick or the prisoner. Have we seen the image of God in Christ in the persons whose burdens were too great for them (Mt. 25:34–45)?

Support Your Teachers (6:6)

Paul is going to return to this theme of our destiny by using the metaphor of sowing and reaping. But he interrupts to say a word about the obligations of the Galatians to those who give of their time and talents in serving by teaching. In his practical way Paul gives an example of how his own teaching can be put into effect. The word for "good things" recalls "the fruit of the Spirit"—goodness/generosity. But he adds here "all" to "good things." He wants to indicate that life in freedom is not only generous, but spontaneous, open–hearted and open–handed, not keeping anything back from those in need, especially those who give of themselves to us. It may be that Paul was delicately reminding the Galatians that they need the benefit of the teaching skills of those best fitted to use them. But this involves generous support in interchurch aid. In his letter to the Corinthians, Paul gives a hint that he had to prod the Galatians to make their contribution for the churches: "Now concerning the collection for the saints: you should follow the directions I gave to the churches of Galatia" (1 Cor. 16:1). This is a shrewd way of telling us that freedom in the Spirit is a down–to–earth commitment to reciprocity.

Sowing and Reaping (6:7–10)

Having put in a plug for his teacher colleagues, Paul resumes his counseling in an air of grave warning. "Do not be deceived." This means: "Do not go or be led astray; do not vacillate, be unstable, or confused." He goes on to say: "God is not mocked." The word for "mock" is "snout." One cannot turn up one's nose at God. One cannot despise God or treat God with contempt. These are strong words. They introduce the whole process of sowing and reaping, so often referred to in the Old Testament.

The prophet Hosea challenged Israel that it had "spurned the good" and had fallen into idolatry. He went on to declare:

For they sow the wind
    and they shall reap the whirlwind.
The standing grain has no heads,
    it shall yield no meal. (Hos. 8:7)

The Book of Proverbs says:

Whoever sows injustice will reap calamity,
    and the rod of anger will fail.
Those who are generous are blessed,
    for they share their bread with the poor. (Prov. 22:8–9)

96

Paul uses an image from peasant life and applies it to our existence: <u>What we sow we reap</u>. Paul expresses himself in a peculiar way in Galatians 5:8, which should be translated literally:

> Whoever sows into the flesh, from the flesh will reap corruption [disintegration, destruction, death]
> Whoever sows into the Spirit, from the Spirit will reap eternal life.

"Flesh" and "Spirit" become like fields and soil in which we sow. We can direct our freedom "into the flesh," into a life of selfishness, self–will and self–indulgence in cynical disregard for God. The inevitable consequence will be disintegration and death. <u>We can direct our freedom "into the Spirit," the life and the power of God in Christ, the blessing</u>. The equally inevitable consequence will be integrating, indestructible, <u>eternal life</u>.

The way to freedom lies clearly before us, if we will be true to our calling. Without weariness, and persistently, we have to tend the soil and the plant of freedom by "doing what is right." A more literal translation of "doing what is right" is "doing the good." The word for "doing" is used in the Greek Old Testament for "create." The word "good," *kalon*, is precisely the translation used in the Greek Old Testament on every major act of creation: "And God saw that it was good," *kalon*, splendid (Gen. 1:12, 18, 21, 25, 31). This word, *kalon*, means both "good" and "beautiful," as well as "effective" and "efficient," accomplishing what was intended. Jesus is the Good Shepherd, *kalos*—one who is beautifully fitted for the task, and does it with consistency and persistence, even to the point of giving his life for the sheep (Jn. 10:7–15). Our freedom in the Spirit, our true spirituality, is a constant, spontaneous, creative act of self–giving love in all its beauty and bounty. So at each opportune moment, let us go on doing the good to all, both near and far, without distinction. Nevertheless, the test of our freedom is <u>the way in which we do good to those who share</u>

our life in Christ with us, with all the difficulties that arise from living intimately in a congregation. There is an old saying: "Charity begins at home." It does not stay there, but it must be practiced there as a sign that all may see, and say, with the Psalmist: "How very good and pleasant it is when kindred live together in unity!" (Ps. 133:1).

Bearing the Marks of Jesus (6:11–18)

Paul has come to the end of a heatedly detailed letter. He has had to assert the freedom and the truth of the gospel. Here he picks up the pen from his letter–writer and, before signing it, sums up the essence of what he had to write.

He cannot refrain from referring to those who have come to disturb the churches of Galatia with their insistence that believers be circumcised. Certainly these trouble–makers will not be persecuted for confessing Christ cruci–fied! How can they, when Christ is not the only Savior for them? They do not even keep the law that they want to impose. They are really only seeking to boast that they have got the Galatians where they want them, but it is "in the flesh," in what perishes and dies.

As for Paul, his one and only boast is "the cross of our Lord Jesus Christ." It is by clinging to this cross that he is crucified to the world, the old creation. The life he now lives in the flesh, he lives by faith in the son of God who loved him and gave himself for him (2:20).

What really matters to Paul now is not circumcision or uncircumcision, but "a new creation." This is his last theo–logical statement in this letter. It is written with his own hand, and bears his own seal. The most astonishing reality for him is what Christ has done for us. He "delivered us from the present evil age" (1:4). He has "redeemed us from the curse of the law" (3:13) and from being "under the law" (4:5). This liberation is the manifestation of God's new creative act in Christ. As he writes to the Corinthians: "If anyone is in Christ, there is a new creation; everything old has passed away; see, everything has become new. All this is from God . . ." (2 Cor. 5:17–18a). The image of God in us is now expressed in a new life in community in which all our relationships are refashioned in a unity in diversity (3:28); we belong to the one family of God as sisters and brothers (4:5–6); our faith in Christ is put to work in love (5:6); we are free persons serving one another in love (5:13–14); we live, are guided by and bear the fruit of the Spirit unto eternal life (5:18, 22–23, 25; 6:8); we bear one another's burdens and do good to all (6:2, 10).

Paul began his letter with the greeting: "Grace and peace." Now he ends, or almost ends, with the blessing: "Peace and mercy." But this time the blessing is addressed to all who walk in step (the verb from *stoicheia*, the elements, comes back again), not in slavery to law or the powers of this world, but in the freedom of knowing and following the *canon*, the rule of faith of the new Israel of God, the community of believers in Christ.

As for Paul himself, he goes on unperturbed, bearing the *stigmata* of Jesus. Daily, the Galatians saw slaves walking on the road carrying burnt marks on their flesh, indicating to whom they belonged. Paul has in this letter opened his breast to the Galatians that they might see the crucified marks of him to whom he belongs—Jesus, who saves and liberates.

"May the grace of our Lord Jesus Christ be with your spirit, brothers and sisters, Amen."

Notes

1. M. Dibelius and W. G. Kummel, *Paul*, (Philadelphia: Westminster Press, 1953), p. 28.
2. Dibelius and Kummel, *Paul*, p. 21.
3. David Gill, Ed., *Gathered into Life*, (Grand Rapids: E.B. Eerdmans, 1983), p. 86.
4. Susanne Heine, *Women in Early Christianity*, (Minneapolis: Augsburg Publishing House, 1988), p. 82.
5. H. D. Betz, *Galatians*, (Philadelphia: Fortress Press, 1984), p. 245.
6. C.K. Barrett, *Freedom and Obligation*, (London: SPCK, 1985), p. 28.
7. John Pobee and Barbel Wartenberg–Potter, *New Eyes for Reading*, (Yorktown Heights, NY: Meyer Stone Books, 1987).
8. J. Neusner, *The Rabbinic Traditions about the Pharisees before 70*, I, (Leiden, 1971), pp. 321–324.
9. Quoted in C.K. Barrett, *Freedom and Obligation*, p. 3.
10. H.D. Betz, *Galatians*, p. 289.
11. E.F. Bruce, *The Epistle to the Galatians*, (Grand Rapids: W. B. Eerdmans, 1988), p. 260.

Books for Further Reading

On Paul
M. Dibelius and W.G. Kummel. *Paul*. Philadelphia: Westminster Press, 1953.
C.H. Dodd. *The Meaning of Paul for Today*. Utica, NY: Meridian Books, 1957.
Lucas Grollenberg. *Paul*. Louisville: Westminster John Knox, 1979.

John Knox. *Chapters in the Life of Paul.* (2nd revised edition) Macon, GA: Mercer U. Press, 1987.

Robin Scroggs. *Paul for a New Day.* Minneapolis: Augsburg Fortress Press, 1977.

Commentaries and Studies on Galatians

C. K. Barrett. *Freedom and Obligation: A Study of the Epistle to the Galatians.* Louisville: Westminster John Knox, 1985.

Hans Dieter Betz. *Galatians.* Minneapolis: Augsburg Fortress Press, 1979.

Charles R. Erdman. *Epistle of Paul to the Galatians.* Louisville: Westminster John Knox, 1976.

Interpreter's Bible, Vol. 10. Section on Galatians. Nashville: Abingdon Press, 1953.

Peter Richardson. *Paul's Ethic of Freedom.* Louisville: Westminster John Knox, 1979.

Frank Stagg. *Galatians and Romans.* Louisville: Westminster John Knox, 1980.

Related Studies

Susanne Heine. *Women and Early Christianity.* Minneapolis: Augsburg Fortress Publishing House, 1988.

John Pobee and Barbel Wartenberg–Potter. *New Eyes for Reading: Biblical and Theological Reflections by Women of the Third World.* Yorktown Heights, New York: Meyer Stone Books, 1987.

Walter Wink. *Naming the Powers: The Language of Power in the New Testament.* Minneapolis: Augsburg Fortress, 1984.

Teacher's Guide to
FREEDOM
IS FOR FREEING
A Study Book on Paul's Letter to the Galatians
by Marilyn Whaley Winters

Contents

Introduction

This is a study about <u>law</u>, <u>faith</u>, and <u>freedom</u>. Paul's letter to the Galatians has a certain historical setting. The early church's struggle was one of defining itself in relation to Judaism since it had its origins within the Jewish community. Paul's letter is addressed to newly formed communities of Christians who have been persuaded by certain other Christians (probably some who grew up in the Jewish tradition) that they should keep the Mosaic law, including the practice of circumcision, just as the Jewish community does. Paul is saying, " No!" and he writes his letter to make his point. Something new has happened in Christ; something all inclusive and universal is taking shape. In the final analysis, it is no less demanding, but it has to do with living by the Spirit. "For freedom, Christ has set us free." (See chapter 1 of the text, the section titled, "Confusion.")

Today's church is not confronted with the same questions that faced the newly emerging churches of Paul's time. We must learn to read Galatians with the understanding that it will speak to us in ways different from the ways it spoke to Christians of Galatia in the first century C.E. Even so, we will discover that it does focus on the disciplines still basic to Christian living —not laws, not rules and regulations — but those disciplines that shape our lives as we learn to "<u>live by the Spirit</u>." (See Galatians 5:22.)

The study book, "Freedom Is for Freeing," is pastoral and testimonial. It will help us see Galatians not only in its historical context but as a message for us today. The authors, Barbel Wartenberg–Potter and Philip Potter, describe themselves in this way:

> *Barbel*: *European,* with its history of dominance (colonial, neo–colonial, economic, theological), *white,* with a history of racism, yet involved in the struggle against racism; with theological formation in the

Lutheran–reformed tradition; *female*, with experience of marginalization within the structure of privilege in the first world; *part of the women's movement*; age: *mid–forties*, having studied in the midst of the student movements of the late sixties.

Philip: *Caribbean*, representing the history of colonized people and slavery, a descendant of European and African ancestry. Strong *Methodist* background; black, with the existential experience of racism and a deep involvement in a struggle against racism; *male*, privileged out of a history of oppression, holding leadership positions in the church at the highest level; *in solidarity with women* in their struggle; age: *mid–sixties*, with an experience of over forty years of active ministry in the ecumenical movement.

Paul, the author of the New Testament letter to the Galatians, could be described in this way:

Paul: An apostle of Jesus Christ and a writer of very personal letters that later become a part of the church's witness to its own life and self–understanding. In his letters, Paul describes his life experience and faith journey. He was passionate in wanting the Galatians to be truly free in Christ.

Overview and Leader Preparation

Read carefully the textbook for this study and the Book of Galatians from the NEW Revised Standard Version of the Bible. (Note that Galatians from the NRSV is printed in its totality in this study. Each chapter of the study begins with a chapter of the book of Galatians.) As you read, recall some historical and personal experiences of freedom that you know about or have experienced, that is, experiences of being freed from past oppressions, past confinements, past systems that enslaved. These reflections and experiences should be recorded during your first reading of the text and your beginning preparation for the study. (Plan to ask all who participate in this study to do the same.)

Also, as you read the book of Galatians, notice all those marvelous sayings of Paul that you have probably read, and even memorized in the past, but have possibly forgotten. They are almost like "mottos" for living. Copy a few of them on poster paper and live with them during this study, letting them renew your spirit and energize you as you think of the challenges facing the church today. (Ask participants in the study to do likewise.)

You will also need to begin to collect current resources from magazines, periodicals, newspapers, and religious publications. Using additional resources of others' struggles for freedom will add depth and validate action in the study.

In addition to the text, the Bible, and current periodicals, you might find it helpful to collect and use supplemental resources from recent mission studies, especially those that deal with oppression and liberation, or with openness to the all–inclusive nature of God's love. Other helpful background readings are listed at the end of both the study and this guide.

Plan for six sessions, using the six chapters of *Freedom Is for Freeing* as a guide. As already noted, the authors have included the biblical text in the study book. The chapter divisions are identified with subtitles for easy reference and summaries. Clarify the purpose of the study and the focus of each session. A review of appropriate methodologies to achieve learning experiences may be helpful and useful. Mark any items in the text and resource materials that you think will be of interest to the study group. Plan which activities and extra resources you will want to use. Be sure to order the resources and recruit necessary volunteers for the study sessions far enough in advance to permit thorough preparation. After making decisions for the overall plan, review the plans for the study sessions.

You will not be able or want to do everything suggested.

Choose what is best for you and the group. As a study leader you will not need to be an "expert" in biblical knowledge; however, it is desirable that you be as familiar as possible with the content of this study in order to guide the study process effectively.

About Worship

This guide does not include detailed suggestions for worship, but when time allows, and it is appropriate, plan to begin your sessions with scripture, hymn singing and prayer. You might close each session with the benediction with which Paul closes his letter to the Galatians: "May the grace of our Lord Jesus Christ be with your spirit . . . Amen."

Session 1

Preparation

Read the Foreword, the Introduction and Chapter 1 of the text, *Freedom Is for Freeing*, along with the first chapter of Galatians.

Wall Displays
Display some pictures of letters or photo essays depicting domestic and global situations that need our attention, as listed in the text. For example:
1. The impulse to assume unlimited growth on a limited earth
2. The destruction of the environment
3. Evidence of devastating poverty of two–thirds of the world's population
4. Sexual abuse
5. Growing crime
6. Deadly diseases
7. Drug abuse
8. Breakup of families
9. Racial and cultural conflicts
10. Loss of hope

Quotations
Quote some appropriate historical and contemporary "apostles," including the statement from Levi Oracion, the Filipino prophet, which appears in the Foreword of this study:

"To be ready for death simplifies one's life, purifies one's soul and gives one tremendous courage. It allows for a radical disengagement with the non–essentials of life and frees one for a total commitment to truth."

Begin a collection of statements that can be added to, for each study session—for example, statements by Martin

Luther King, Jr., John Wesley, Dame Nita Barrow, Bishop Leontine Kelly, Howard Thurman, Elsa Tamez, Julia Esquival, courageous priests, poets, pastors, political leaders —women and men— from various parts of the globe. These might be paired with quotations from the book of Galatians, such as:

It is no longer I who live, but it is Christ who lives in me. (2:20)

There is no longer Jew or Greek, there is no longer slave or free, there is no longer male and female; for all of you are one in Christ Jesus. (3:28)

But when the fullness of time had come, God sent his Son, born of a woman, born under the law, in order to redeem those who were under the law, so that we might receive adoption as children. (4:4–5)

You, my friends, are children of the promise. (4:28)

For freedom, Christ has set us free. (5:1)

For you were called to freedom, brothers and sisters, only do not use your freedom as an opportunity for self–indulgence. . . . (5:13)

The whole law is summed up in a single commandment, "You shall love your neighbor as yourself." (5:14)

Live by the Spirit (5:16)

The fruit of the spirit is love, joy, peace, patience, kindness, generosity, faithfulness, gentleness, and self–control. (5:22)

Bear one another's burdens. (6:2)

All must carry their own loads. (6:5)

Do not be deceived; God is not mocked, for you reap whatever you sow. (6:7)

So, let us not grow weary in doing what is right. . . . (6:9)

A new creation is everything. (6:15b)

May the grace of our Lord Jesus Christ be with your spirit, brothers and sisters. Amen. (6:18)

Visualchart

Prepare a visualchart to describe Paul, the churches in Galatia and the letter.

Galatia:
Churches in Galatia:
Paul Hellenistic Jew: Roman Citizen: Pharisee:
The Letter Time: Theme: Style: Content:

The Session

1. Introduce the text, the additional resources and the study process.

2. Begin by asking each person to reflect on the questions posed by the authors about letters and letterwriting. Allow a few minutes for participants to write down their responses. Then ask people to discuss in small groups what they have written. Allow a few minutes for this and then share the results in the larger group. Highlight as a group some of the learnings from the refections.

3. Brief presentation by leader (or participants alerted to prepare in advance) on the content in the Introduction using the visualchart describing Galatia, the churches in Galatia, and the letter. Your church library will probably contain a Bible dictionary or atlas with maps of the region of Galatia that would also be useful.

4. Ask the group to spend a few minutes reflecting on and then writing about being "set free from the present evil age." (Gal. 1:4) Then invite them to share with one another, one on one, some of their reflections.

5. Discuss this quotation from the authors' "Letter to Our Readers":
   "As Christians we are not promised comfortable paths. What we are promised is that God will be beside us on our way. And there is more "life in life if we do not avoid its depths and heights, but "choose life" (Deut. 30:19).

6. Ask the group to sit quietly and to reflect for a few minutes on the question: What was your conversion experience? Give this assignment to groups of three persons each:
   a) Silently read Bärbel's witness regarding conversion in chapter 1.
   b) Share three points made by Bärbel with which you can agree.

c)   If possible, respond to Barbel's question: What is your experience? As one person in each group speaks, the other two persons in the group should listen, saving their questions for the end of the presentation. Ask questions for clarification only. Statements and comments in this exercise should not be judgmental.

7.   The text helps us to understand God's call to Paul. Paul understood through his encounters with Christ that a new way of life had been opened for all humanity. Discuss the following statement made by Barbel in her description of her "conversion": "One thing is clear: A true conversion always leaves recognizable traces behind. Suddenly or slowly, life turns in another direction."

8.   Paul emphasizes that he is part of a missionary team. Note Galatians 1:2. Discuss chapter 1 of the text. Encourage everyone to read it if they have not done so already. Use the slide set for the study if you have ordered it from the Service Center. (See Additional Resources, p. 128.)

9.   Make assignments for next session (see Preparation for session 2).

10. Close the session with a unison reading of Galatians 6:18.

Assignment: Invite volunteers to work with you in preparing a panel discussion on "A Difficult Meeting" and "Remember the Poor" based on material from chapter 2 of the text book. Ask all participants to read chapter 2.

Session 2

Preparation

Reread chapter 2 of the text book, "Conflict in the Church," including chapter 2 of Galatians.

Scan some of the resources on poverty, global and domestic, that you collected as you prepared for this study. It is important in this session to have resources available to the group that illustrate the ways of "doing theology" given in chapter 2 of the study book. Try to find examples of witness letters written by such people as Dietrich Bonhoeffer, Gandhi, Martin Luther King, Jr., and/or witness letters from Guatemala and Philippines, South Africa and Korea to be shared with the group. (See Resources.)

In advance, ask for volunteers to help you prepare exhibits that give contemporary expression to the Christian faith, using art and creative work as suggested by Bärbel Wartenburg–Potter in her statement on "doing theology."

Display some pictures, photo essays or posters that depict domestic and global poverty.

Write verse 20 on newsprint or chalkboard so that it can be read at the close of the session. If you can locate a copy of *The Gospel in Solentiname* by Ernesto Cardinal ask two participants to prepare a dialogue report on it. (See Resources. Although there are four volumes, the introduction is the same in all four volumes.)

The Session

Begin the session by reviewing for the group the important points made by the authors in chapter 2 of the study of Galatians. Then, choose from the suggestions that follow activities that you think would be appropriate for your group.

1. Ask participants to read their choice of a witness letter, giving background information about the person and the situation that caused the letter to be written.

2. Organize a panel discussion that helps the group to acknowledge and understand conflict and confrontation in the church. (See assignment at close of session 1.) Also, to internalize the perception that deprivation and degrading human conditions

should compel the Christian community to action. When the panel has concluded, divide into small groups to identify discussion questions, reconvene and raise the questions with the panel.

3. Ask the group to look at photographs of poverty. In one–on–one communications, talk about feelings of guilt and helplessness. What are some of the ways we can deal with this guilt? Allow time for this discussion. Join two more persons and discuss: What are the basic fears that make us reject people for whose problems we have no solutions? How are affluence and poverty in our world related?

4. Ask the group to reread the story of the rich young man, Mark 10:17–31, and the comments made by Bärbel Wartenburg–Potter in chapter 2 of the study, in the witness statement, titled, "Who Are the Poor Today?"

   In groups of three, discuss the questions raised about poverty. How can wealth be shared? Can exploitation be stopped? Identify examples in your discussion.

5. Mother Teresa made the statement, "Jesus comes among us today disguised as the poor." Do you agree with this statement?

6. What does this mean for the mission and ministry of the church and for faithful Christians?

7. Allow time for reports and presentations or exhibits, illustrating "doing theology by art and creative work."

8. The authors tell us that Galatians 2:20 has had a profound effect on many Christians. They mention Martin Luther as an example. What meaning does this verse have for you? (Does it mean that you give up your unique self–identity or does it mean that your unique self is both informed and transformed by Christ within?) Reflect for a few moments and share your thoughts in your groups of three.

9. For closure, ask one person in the group to read verse 20 aloud while another copies it on newsprint; then ask the total group to read the verse silently from the newsprint. For your benediction, read Galatians 6:18.

Assignment: Careful reading and rereading of chapter 3.

Session 3

Preparation

Reread chapter 3, "Now That Faith Has Come," and find resources related to the section, "Breaking Down Barriers." Display a "Freedom Is for Freeing" mural or collage of contemporary "apostles" using pictures and quotes. Be sure to include women and persons of a variety of racial and ethnic groups.

Chapter 3 stresses the importance of the crucifixion and God's identification through it with the poor. One commentator on this study observed, "The shocking death of Jesus cannot be divorced from his shocking life." She added: "The spirit is given to all even when the works of law can only be understood by the scholars."

As the authors point out in chapter 3, there is a thanksgiving morning prayer in which a male Jew thanks God that he was not made a Gentile, a slave or a woman. In U.S. folklore, there is a singsong: "If you're white, you're right; if you're brown, stick around; if you're black, get back!" Galatians 3:28 is a radical re–ordering of such thinking.

The task for this session is to struggle with how radically we take the freedom that Christ gives us. The assignment is for the study group to prepare and design the group experience. Allow time for this exercise.

The Session

Step 1.   Assign small groups to list from three to five concepts from this chapter that could be discussed by the total group. Include some from the contemporary witness statements. (See Table of Contents.)

Step 2.   Ask the small groups to exchange with each other their lists and why they chose them.

Step 3.   By pooling all the suggestions, combining some, selecting from the total list, design a discussion plan for this session.

Step 4.   Assign one or two questions to a small group of three or four persons for discussion.

Step 5.   Ask the small groups to share their responses with the whole group. If possible, put the findings on newsprint so that the report can be posted during the remainder of the study sessions.

Some possible topics:

If the group needs help in searching out "concepts" or "questions" from the study book, chapter 3, ask the following as they work:

● What does Paul mean by "foolish" when he calls the Galatians foolish in 3:1–5.

● How are the words, "righteousness," "blessing," and "faith" used in both the Genesis and Galatians passages as described in chapter 3?

● Why do you think Paul is so agitated about whether circumcision is necessary? Is he saying the law is not necessary? Or is he describing a way of fulfilling the law that is quite different from what was commonly understood in his day? See if you can explain the difference. For instance: How would you rewrite the Ten Commandments (Genesis 20:2ff or Deuteronomy 5:6ff) if you were trying to express what it means to live by the Spirit of the law?

● What is this freedom we have in Christ?

- How does Paul see the promise to Abraham being fulfilled in Christ?
- What is the significance of baptism as the chosen sign of the new creation?

Galatians 3:28 has been called by the authors of this study the Magna Charta of the Christian faith. Notice its construction: no longer Jew *or* Greek, no longer slave *or* free, no longer male *and* female. Why "or" with Jew or Greek, slave or free, but "and" with male and female? Is Paul trying to imply something different here about equality? About oneness in Christ? Some think that in the early church there was a radical break away from the traditional roles lived out by men and women in the cultures of that time, and that this was an early Christian creed already in effect, which Paul is simply quoting. Some think it implies much more equality of roles as teachers, preachers, leaders than was later the case when a kind of male dominance re–asserted itself in the life of the church. Review again the slide set for *Freedom Is for Freeing* if time allows. (See Additional Resources, p. 128.)

Bring this session to a close with a brief period of worship, using the benediction of Galatians 6:18.

Assignment: Careful reading and rereading of chapter 4.

Session 4

Preparation

Reread chapter 4, "Coming of Age." Paul continues to pull out all the stops in chapter 4 to talk about the freedom we have in Christ. He argues that we are not victims of the elements. He argues that the Galatians are somewhat like children who lived as slaves until they came into their own inheritance in Christ. He uses the Genesis story of Sarah and Hagar to talk of the difference between being children of slavery and children of the Spirit. The authors of the Bible study struggle with all these points, and take issue with Paul to some extent. Paul's basic point, however, is simply this: we are not bound by "capricious gods" or the law, but are children of a loving God, children of the promise, free in Christ.

In chapter 4, try to outline for yourself (or summarize) the authors' description of "the elements" as they were understood in Paul's time, and as we understand them today. (See the section, "Under Guardians and Powers.") Be prepared to talk about this with the study group. The authors write: "People [in Paul's time] were ruled by fear and Fate and Fortune, considered to be capricious gods. So religion flourished — not only the old local pagan cults, but new ones called mystery religions, as well as mixtures of all." Does this sound like today's culture? What are today's "mystery religions"? What do people rely on to help them "make it" through the day, through life?

What is the difference between making "capricious gods" of the elements and finding in the elements channels for being in touch with the Spirit? For instance, women tend to respond to signs and symbols. We like the idea that a rock can remind us of the mystery and presence of God in creation and that a small pebble held in one's hand can somehow evoke a relationship with God's creation, and therefore with God. The rock does not become God. The rock is simply a felt awareness that God is Creator in ways beyond our ever comprehending, and that there is something "sacred" about this world that has been given to us. Think of other ways that "the elements" become means of recognizing the Spirit, not substitutes for it.

Another theme of this chapter is that of Paul's concern about the Galatians being like children. The first seven verses speak of children who cannot claim their inheritance until they come of age. Then, later, Paul speaks of "my little children, with whom I am in the pain of childbirth until

Christ is formed in you" (4:19). Be prepared to discuss Paul as spiritual"father" and also spiritual "mother" to the Galatians. (See "Pains of Childbirth.")

Read carefully the authors' comments on the Sarah/ Hagar story, including Bärbel's "witness statement." Make preparations for the group to participate in a discussion of Paul's use of this story and Bärbel's observations about it in light of our sensitivity to women's issues today, and to people of races and cultures other than our own. Would you like to argue with Paul about his use of the Sarah/Hagar story? Do you identify with Sarah or Hagar or both? Plan to discuss these questions in your group session. (See Resources.)

The Session

1. Ask the group to look up the Genesis story of Sarah and Hagar, referred to in the text. (See the chart on Hagar and Sarah in the text. Note also the scripture references just above the chart.) Ask half the group to reconstruct the story and prepare to tell it from Sarah's point of view. Ask the other half to prepare and present the story from Hagar's point of view. Allow plenty of time for this activity. Also, allow time for discussion, after each presentation, of the themes and issues that the story raises, such as racism, refugees, agism, the impossible being done through God, abused spouses or abused children, competition.

2. If time allows, discuss "the elements" based on material in the text and comments made in the "Preparation" section.

3. Close this session by having someone in the group who attended the Assembly of United Methodist Women, in Kansas City, in May,describe the use of small rocks at the Assembly and how the rocks became symbols of God's intimacy, God's presence with us in all of creation. If no one from your church attended the Assembly, simply

discuss briefly among yourselves the difference between being "enslaved to beings that by nature are not gods" (4:8) and using signs, symbols, things, (the stars, the cross, a flower, balloons, an icon, special days and seasons of the church year), as means of evoking one's awareness of the Spirit of God in our midst. Use Galatians 6:18 as the benediction.

Assignment: Ask each person in the group to prepare her own witness statement using the authors' format. See the Table of Contents for the list of witness statements. The witness statement could be a response to any part of Paul's letter to the Galatians. Encourage participants to plan on sharing their witness statement. In addition, for the next session, all participants should read chapter 5.

Session 5

Preparation

Reread chapter 5, "Freedom in the Spirit." The theme of this session is freedom!

Post quotes on newsprint or chalkboard:

Martin Luther: "The will of a person without grace is not free, but slavish." . . . "A Christian is the most free Lord of all, and subject to none. A Christian is the most willing servant of all and subject to everyone."(*Freedom Is for Freeing*, chapter 5)

Karl Jaspers: "No one is free who does not work for the freedom of others." (*Freedom Is for Freeing*, chapter 5)

Billy Taylor:
"I wish I knew how it would feel to be free
I wish I could break all those chains holding me
I wish I could say all the things I should say
Say 'em loud, say 'em clear, for the whole world to
hear!"

Words to the spiritual:
". . . and before I'll be a slave,
I'll be buried in my grave
and go home to my Lord and be free!"

In advance of the session, ask one of the participants to be prepared to tell the story told by Philip Potter in his witness statement on the liberation of the Caribbean in 1834 and how the Galatians 5 text was used in that context.

Consider the possibility of showing one of the recommended films listed in Resources at the end of the study. Post the "Commitment and Action" questions on newsprint/chalkboard. If equipment is available, the questions could be photocopied for each participant. (See p. 123.)

The Session

1. Ask how individuals are doing in their preparation of witness statements, using the format of the authors in chapter 4. If several persons have completed their statements, ask them to share with the group
2. Summarize (or ask volunteers to do so) the basic content of chapter 5.
3. Focus on the familiar verses about the works of the flesh and the fruit of the spirit. Review the points made by the authors in the section titled. "Living by the Spirit or the Flesh?"

After listing the fruit of the Spirit of Galatians 5:22, Robin Scrogg in a little book titled *Paul for a New Day*

(Philadelphia: Fortress, 1977), observes: "What a list of unaggressive, loving, caring values. And do I need point out that in any sexist handbook these would be labeled 'feminine virtues'? For Paul they are descriptions of all human eschatological persons!" (p. 37.)

Scroggs is suggesting that in our culture the attributes we extoll as fruit of the Spirit have been consigned to women, while Paul is saying that *all* persons who claim to be a part of the new creation should be persons of *love, joy, peace, patience, kindness, goodness, faithfulness, gentleness,* and *self control*. Talk about this.

And what about the works of the flesh? (Check the authors' definition of what Paul means by works of the flesh in chapter 5.) Are the works Paul lists in Galatians forms of behavior that we often attribute to men more than women? How would you describe the works of the flesh as they pertain to women? Which ones from Paul's list would you include? What other "works of the flesh" would you add?

4. If you decided to use a video, this might be the appropriate time to do so."
   Allow time for discussion:
   • *Question*: How does the theme of our study, "Freedom Is for Freeing" relate to the issues of this film?

Close this session with a period of sentence prayers for persons seeking freedom today. Sing "I Wish I Knew How It Would Feel to Be Free" and the spiritual printed at the beginning of this session.

Assignment: For the last session, in addition to reading the final chapter of Galatians and the final chapter of the text, focus on the phrase, "a new creation is everything" (6:15b). What would a new creation look like? Would you be willing to try to "map it out" by using the questions that follow?

How Can I Become a Part of
THE NEW CREATION?

(Preparation for the faith journey in a new decade)
Statement of Commitment and Action

What will a New Creation look like?

What will help it to happen?

What would *I* like to see happen in the next decade?

How Can I help it happen?

What will my struggles be?

What will hinder me?

When will I start?

Session 6

Reread chapter 6, "Bear One Another's Burdens," reflecting on and marking for emphasis the sections that have to do with freedom, and the responsibility that goes with it. Note that in the section titled, "Freed from the Yoke of Slavery," the authors say:

"We either grow in freedom or we fall back into the slavery of legalism or licentious living or both."

Note also Thomas Jefferson's claim:

"The price of liberty is eternal vigilance."

Plan to print these, and other quotes from the chapter, on newsprint and place them on the walls of the meeting room for this session. Note particularly the section in the text, "Bearing the Marks of Jesus." Review the video "Mama, I'm Crying," produced by Joyce Seroke and Betty Wolpert. (See Resources for film description and information for ordering. Be sure to order well in advance.) Plan time for viewing the video.

Ask the group to share poems, prayers, or stories from the study book or their supplemental readings. Encourage the use of *Churches in Solidarity with Women* (see Resources) or resources from previous mission studies. Encourage group members to be prepared to share their witness statements. Plan to allow time for completion of reflection/action plan "A New Creation."

Notice how this last session builds on the one that just preceded it. Ask someone to be prepared to read the section in chapter 6 that defines "faith" (if possible, have copies made of this statement to give to each participant in the study).

Plan appropriate closing for study session.

The Session

1. Discuss the authors' interpretation of 6:3–4. How does the phrase, "Bear one another's burdens" relate to the phrase, "All should carry their own load"?
2. Ask for the reading of the following section on faith, which you assigned in advance to a participant:

". . . Paul is very wisely and skillfully helping us to understand what freedom is all about. We are liberated by Christ from all that prevents us from being ourselves as persons made in God's image, and as unique individuals having beauty, dignity and indestructible value. The guidance of the Spirit enables us to discern what the choices in life are, in the course of our concrete, daily movements and encounters. But it is we who have to decide, we who have to respond to our situation in a responsible way. *It is this responding and responsibility that is called "faith" in the Bible.* It is the free, voluntary decision to be faithful, reliable, committed. It is our capacity to say *Amen* to the God before whom we live: 'I believe you; I put myself, my life at your disposal.' "

Ask the group to form small groups of two or three and discuss:
a) What did you have to be "liberated from" that was preventing you from being a person made in God's image, unique, having beauty, dignity, indestructible value?
b) Recall a time when you had to make a difficult choice in a "responding, responsible" way that you would call "faith."

3. If you have decided to use the video, "Mama, I'm Crying,"this might be an appropriate time to do so, asking the viewers to think about what faith meant to the women portrayed in the video as they view their stories.

4. Ask the group to reread and reflect on the section in the text, "Bearing the Marks of Jesus."
5. Share with the total group: quotations from chapter 6 of the text, or chapter 6 of Galatians, or selected poems, prayers, stories, and witness statements. Design such sharing so that it all becomes a part of a closing worship experience.

Resources

Suggested Film/Video

Homeland—The narration for the film, *Homeland*, was inspired by a famous speech made in 1855 by Chief Seattle, the well–known leader of the Duwamish tribe of Native Americans. (The city of Seattle, Washington, was named for him.) The United States government wanted to buy land from Chief Seattle, and in his speech, the chief was trying to communicate the Indians' feelings and attachment for their land. The original speech has been expanded for the film, but the additions remain true to Chief Seattle's basic philosophy. 16mm color film, 21 minutes, Counterpoint Films, 1977. Rental, $20.

Bonhoeffer: A Life of Challenge—The film is divided between reflective tributes from friends, colleagues and admirers, and a dynamic view of Bonhoeffer's life as shaped by his constant inquiry: Who is Christ?

Interviews offer a rare and perhaps unequaled opportunity to know Bonhoeffer through those who loved and worked with him. Jean Lasserre recalls their years at Union Theological Seminary; Eberhard Bethge, his biographer, recalls how he courageously set out to recheck the Reformation tradition; Robert Hawthorne illuminates his life as a blend of two ideas—the difficulty of Christian faith, and the theology of taking on others' suffering.

Rare photographs help form a personal biography confirming the observation of Bishop Albrecht Schonherr that Bonhoeffer's writings alone do not reveal the whole man. Among the highlights of his "hidden" life are the years of studies at Tubingen and in America and his bold choice to participate in the plots on Hitler's life. The witness of Bonhoeffer's death confirms his wish that the words of Christ be heard over the chaos of history. 16mm color, 28 minutes. Heritage Media, 1979. Rental, $35.

Homeland and *Bonhoeffer* are available from Ecufilm, an ecumenical film/video distribution service. To order call toll free 1–800–251–4091, or write Ecufilm, 810 Twelfth Ave. South, Nashville, TN 37203

Mama, I'm Crying contrasts the attitudes towards change of two generations in South Africa. It begins as a personal journey of two friends, now middle aged. Joyce Seroke is black; Betty Wolpert is white. Both were born in Johannesburg and their fathers worked for a mining company. Yet they might as well have come from different countries, so different was their experience growing up. As they reflect on the injustices towards blacks they have witnessed, they recall that their generation expected change to come about peacefully and slowly. But today the young people they know are no longer able to accept humiliation and oppression. Among these is twenty-one–year–old Benjamin Olipant whose yearning to live and passion for justice shines through the film. But so too does his prediction that he will be killed. He represents thousands of young people in South Africa who are willing to sacrifice their lives in the passionate belief that justice will prevail.

Video. Available from Film–Makers, 124 40 St., New York, N.Y. 10016. Rental: $75 per showing. Purchase price: $195. (Phone: (212) 808–4980.)

Additional Resources

1. *Ecumenical Decade: The Churches in Solidarity with Women, 1988–1998. Prayers and Poems, Songs and Stories*
WCC Publications, Order from the U.S. Office, World Council of Churches, Room 1062, 475 Riverside Dr., New York, NY 10115.
The Ecumenical Decade of Churches in Solidarity with Women aims at:
   - empowering women to challenge oppressive structures in the global community, their country and their church;
   - affirming—through shared leadership and decision–making theology and spirituality—the decisive contributions of women in churches and communities;
   - giving visibility to women's perspectives and actions in the work and struggle for justice, peace and the integrity of creation;
   - enabling the churches to free themselves from racism, sexism and classism; from teachings and practices that discriminate against women;
   - enabling the churches to take actions in solidarity with women.

   The prayers, poems, songs and stories are expressions from women all over the world. The texts reflect the differences and strengths of women. The book may be used as a worship or discussion resource.
2. *The United Methodist Hymnal*, 1989. Freedom and liberation songs are listed in the index, p. 941. Order from The United Methodist Publishing House, 201 Eighth Ave. S., Nashville, TN. 37202
3. *Freedom Is for Freeing* Slide Set with script prepared by the Women's Division, available at the Service Center.

Books as Resources

1. Peggy Billings, *Acting Out Our Conversion*. Women's Division, 1974, available at the Service Center.
2. Allan Boesak, *Walking on Thorns*, RISK Book Series, WCC. (See U.S. address above.) Also Erdman's, 1984.
3. Dietrich Bonhoeffer, *Letters and Papers from Prison*. New York: Macmillan, 1972.
4. John Temple Bristow, *What Paul Really Said about Women*. San Francisco: Harper & Row, 1988.
5. Ernesto Cardinal, *The Gospel in Solentiname*. Vols. 1, 2, 3 and 4. New York: Orbis, 1982
6. Martin Luther King, Jr. and Coretta King, *The Words of Martin Luther King, Jr.* New York: Newmarket, 1985.
7. Howard A. Snyder, *The Radical Wesley*. Grand Rapids: Zondervan, 1987.
8. Howard Thurman, *Deep River*. Richmond, Indiana: Friends United, 1975.

Marilyn Whaley Winters is chairperson of the Board of Directors, Scarritt–Bennett Center, Nashville. She has degrees from Bennett College and Boston University.

Marilyn is a former director of the General Board of Global Ministries. As such, she served as vice president of the Women's Division and chairperson of its Section of Christian Social Relations. She has held roles of leadership in United Methodist Women and been a study leader for schools of Christian Mission. She lives in Southern California.